Ten Ingredients *for a* Joyous Life *and a* Peaceful Home

T0163066

Ten Ingredients *for a* Joyous Life *and a* Peaceful Home

A Spiritual Memoir

by Angela Shelf Medearis,
The Kitchen Diva!
with
Pastor Salem Robinson, Jr.

LAKE ISLE PRESS NEW YORK

Published by:
Lake Isle Press, Inc.
16 West 32nd Street, Suite 10-B
New York, NY 10001
(212) 273-0796
E-mail: lakeisle@earthlink.net

Distributed to the trade by:
National Book Network, Inc.
4501 Forbes Boulevard, Suite 200
Lanham, MD 20706
1(800) 462-6420
www.nbnbooks.com

Library of Congress Control Number: 2009924354

ISBN-13: 978-1-891105-40-1

This book is available at special sales discounts for bulk purchases as premiums or
special editions, including customized covers. For more information, contact the
publisher at (212) 273-0796 or by e-mail, lakeisle@earthlink.net

First edition
Printed in the United States of America

10 9 8 7 6 5 4 3 2 1

Angela's Dedication: In memory of Deacon Lonnie Lee Melton, our brother in Christ, friend, and beloved Sunday School teacher and Charles Leslie Medearis, my father-in-law, who was so proud of everything Michael and I accomplished in Christ and who supported our dreams.

Pastor Robinson's Dedication: To my beautiful wife, Patricia, who is my visual reminder of how much I am loved by God. To my sons, who have given me the joy of fatherhood. I thank God for the enriched life that I have enjoyed by having you still close enough to draw strength from your love. I dedicate this book to my wife and family—you are my divine inspiration here on earth.

Acknowledgments: This book would not have been possible without the miraculous changes that Jesus Christ has made in my life. I want to thank my husband, Michael, and my daughter, Deanna—my favorite editors—both of whom spent many long, late hours polishing this book and listening to me read passages aloud, and whose love, laughter, and support enable me to fulfill my dreams. I also want to thank my son, Lorenzo, and my grandchild, Anysa, both of whom I love dearly and who are my favorite teenagers.

I want to thank Pastor Salem Robinson, Jr., for his contributions and support. This book is inspired by his stellar life in Christ, his wonderful sermons and Bible study lessons, and his biblical counsel for me and for my family. Thank you for allowing the Lord to use you in His service to impact the lives of others. A special thank you goes to First Lady Patricia M. Robinson for her friendship and her wonderful example of a Christian wife and mother. I also want to thank my parents, Howard and Angeline Shelf, our extended family, and my church family at Dunn's Memorial in Austin, Texas for their prayers and support.

Much love and thanks to all of you!
Angela Shelf Medearis, 2008

A special thanks goes to Angela Shelf Medearis for demonstrating the courage to follow the convictions of her faith. I feel very fortunate to have shared a lifelong friendship with such a wonderful person. Where would we be without people like Angela who spice up our lives with genuine faith, love, compassion, and humor?
Pastor Salem Robinson, Jr., 2008

We would also like to thank the staff at Lake Isle Press for having the courage to undertake this project.

We give heartfelt thanks to all of our Brothers and Sisters in Christ at Dunn's Memorial who contributed their testimonies and poems for inclusion in this book:

Sis. Dynisha Cole
Bro. Patric Davidson
Sis. Essi Eargle
Bro. Gary Eargle
Sis. Terri Hargrove
Sis. Anysa Medearis-Bailey
Sis. Deanna Medearis
Bro. Michael Medearis
Sis. Kerissa Mitchell
Sis. Diane Nunn

Sis. Ruby Nunn
Deacon David Oshoko, Sr.
Bro. David Oshoko, Jr.
Deaconess Lutrecia Oshoko
Bro. Walter Petitt
Sis. Nedia Robinson
First Lady Patricia M. Robinson
Bro. Salem "Trey" Robinson, III
Bro. Timothy Robinson

Editor's Note: All scripture references are taken from the King James Version of the Bible.

Contents

Introduction
Angela Shelf Medearis

The Secret Ingredient
Angela Shelf Medearis

Introduction
Pastor Salem Robinson, Jr.

Chapter One: Love
ANGELA'S TESTIMONY
COMMENTS BY PASTOR SALEM ROBINSON, JR.
PASTOR ROBINSON'S SUNDAY SCHOOL LESSON
LOVE
Sis. Essi Eargle

Chapter Two: Forgiveness
ANGELA'S TESTIMONY
COMMENTS BY PASTOR SALEM ROBINSON, JR.
PASTOR ROBINSON'S SUNDAY SCHOOL LESSON

Chapter Three: Service
ANGELA'S TESTIMONY
COMMENTS BY PASTOR SALEM ROBINSON, JR.
PASTOR ROBINSON'S SUNDAY SCHOOL LESSON
USING MY MUSICAL TALENT FOR JESUS CHRIST
Bro. Walter D. Petitt

USING MY GIFTS AND TALENTS FOR THE LORD
Bro. Trey Robinson

Chapter Four: Overcoming Fear

ANGELA'S TESTIMONY

COMMENTS BY PASTOR SALEM ROBINSON, JR.

PASTOR ROBINSON'S SUNDAY SCHOOL LESSONS

I SAY BRING IT ON
Sis. Essi Eargle

OVERCOMING FEAR
Sis. Terri C. Hargrove

Chapter Five: Healing

ANGELA'S TESTIMONY

COMMENTS BY PASTOR SALEM ROBINSON, JR.

PASTOR ROBINSON'S SUNDAY SCHOOL LESSON

A LIVING MIRACLE!
Bro. David Oshoko

Chapter Six: Friendship

ANGELA'S TESTIMONY

COMMENTS BY PASTOR SALEM ROBINSON, JR.

PASTOR ROBINSON'S SUNDAY SCHOOL LESSON

BROTHERS AND SISTERS IN CHRIST
Sis. Essi Eargle

Chapter Seven: Single Christian Relationships

ANGELA'S TESTIMONY

COMMENTS BY PASTOR SALEM ROBINSON, JR.

PASTOR ROBINSON'S SUNDAY SCHOOL LESSON

A SINGLE MALE CHRISTIAN IN HIGH SCHOOL
Bro. David Oshoko, Jr.

A SINGLE FEMALE CHRISTIAN IN HIGH SCHOOL
Sis. Anysa Medearis-Bailey

A Single Christian in College
Sis. Kerissa Mitchell

A Single Christian Parent
Sis. Deanna Medearis

How the Lord Blessed Me as a Single Christian Parent
Sis. Diane Nunn

Life as a Single Christian Male
Bro. Kilpatric Davidson

Dating as a Male Christian
Bro. Gary Eargle

Dating as a Female Christian
Sis. Essi Eargle

Chapter Eight: Christian Marriage

Angela's Testimony

Comments by Pastor Salem Robinson, Jr.

Pastor Robinson's Sunday School Lesson

My Testimony of Marital Harmony
First Lady Patricia M. Robinson

A Blended Family in Christ
Deaconess Lutrecia Oshoko

A Christian Marriage
Bro. Michael Medearis

Chapter Nine: Godly Children

Angela's Testimony

Comments by Pastor Salem Robinson, Jr.

Pastor Robinson's Sunday School Lesson

Raising Godly Children
First Lady Patricia M. Robinson

Raising Children through God
  Bro. Michael Medearis

Growing Up as a Preacher's Kid
  Bro. Timothy Robinson

Life as a Young Mother
  Sis. Nedia Robinson

The Making of a Mother
  Sis. Dynisha Cole

A Mother's Heart
  Sis. Dynisha Cole

Chapter Ten: Faith in Financial Freedom
Angela's Testimony
Comments by Pastor Salem Robinson, Jr.
Pastor Robinson's Sunday School Lesson
Becoming Financially Free
  Sis. Ruby Nunn

Epilogue
  Angela Shelf Medearis

Introduction
Angela Shelf Medearis

Christianity and cooking have a lot in common. You have to understand and include all the ingredients in order to be successful. I believe that there are ten key "ingredients" in the Bible—love, forgiveness, service, overcoming fear, healing, friendship, single Christian relationships, Christian marriage, godly children, and faith. *Ten Ingredients for a Joyous Life and a Peaceful Home: A Spiritual Memoir* is a spiritual guide to incorporating these scriptural elements into your daily life. My hope is that this book will also be a daily affirmation and study guide, as well as a source of strength and inspiration for anyone who wants to live a joyous life and have a peaceful home.

I decided to write this book as a way of sharing what the Lord has done for me in my life. He has blessed me with many gifts, but writing and cooking are two of my favorites. It's no wonder that a woman who is known as the Kitchen Diva would use cooking as a metaphor for Christianity. I love cooking for people because it makes them happy and satisfies their hunger. This book is a spiritual meal that I've prepared for you. I'm praying that what I write will satisfy that craving for peace in your life and that you will be filled with the joy that comes from knowing the Lord and serving Him.

I'm also writing this book because I've been abundantly blessed through the word of God to live a life I could only dream about as a child. My blessings are directly related to my acceptance of Jesus Christ as my personal savior; developing my own personal relationship with Christ through experience; studying the Bible and applying it to my life; my marriage to my husband, Michael; becoming a mother, a grandmother, and a friend; being taught the word of God by precept and example by my pastor, Salem Robinson, Jr.; and embarking on a journey of faith to create a business that is devoted to spreading the gospel of Jesus Christ through the media.

Throughout this book, I use my own testimony and personal experiences to explain what each ingredient means to me. This book is an autobiographical look at my life in Christ. I was blessed to accept Christ at the age of eighteen, so my entire adult life has been spent as a Christian. I've enjoyed writing about my early years as a Christian, the things I've learned as a wife and a mother, the start of my career as a writer, the joys and sorrows of becoming the owner of a multimedia production company, and my struggles to host and produce a television cooking show. Every experience, whether good or seemingly bad, has shaped my life in Christ.

In addition to my testimony, Pastor Robinson provides insightful commentary based on the Bible and scriptural references that further explain the topic of each chapter. Some of my favorite sermons are on Pastor Robinson's website, www.dunnsmemorial.com. They've absolutely changed my life.

I've also included the poems and testimonies of Christians I've known and admired and incorporated them into the appropriate chapters. Whether the poems and testimonies are about finding love or overcoming fear, living a Christian life in high school from a teenager's perspective, or a retiree's viewpoint on obtaining financial freedom using biblical principles—their experiences in Christ are moving and powerful.

This isn't a very big book, but it is powerful because it is honest and it is true. With the help of the Lord, I've tried to express how the word of God has impacted my life, changed me, and filled me with an unspeakable inner joy, no matter how bad things may seem outwardly. My hope is that no matter what emotions this book may evoke in you, you find the ingredients you need to live a joyous and a peaceful life.

Thank the Lord for you!

Angela Shelf Medearis, The Kitchen Diva!
www.divapro.com

The Secret Ingredient
ANGELA SHELF MEDEARIS

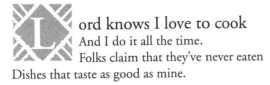ord knows I love to cook
And I do it all the time.
Folks claim that they've never eaten
Dishes that taste as good as mine.

They always want to know my secret
So, I've written cookbooks and recipes by the dozens
Filled with exotic ingredients from near and far,
And simple dishes created by my Mama and my cousins.

I was taught to cook by elderly women
Who never used a recipe
Who taught me by example
About how to love and care for a family.

I've also learned the culinary arts
From famous chefs all dressed in white
Who have their very own cooking shows
That come on television every night.

And still, I've learned when it comes to cooking
It's not the cost of the ingredients that you use,
Or how you hold a butcher knife,
Or the utensils that you choose.

It's not the level of education
That a person may possess,
Or how much is in their bank account,
Or how they choose to dress.

I've learned that food tastes best
When you prepare it with lots and lots of love
And when you give thanks BEFORE you start to cook
To God and Christ above.

I pray before I plan my menu,
Or find the recipes, or start to shop.
I pray while I prepare the ingredients,
And while I stir, and taste, and chop.

I know that food is a powerful way
To express the love of God in simplicity.
And when a meal is extra tasty
Well, honey, that's just God using me.

Sometimes folks need a little extra love
In a way they can understand
And food is a universal language
Understood by every woman, child, and man.

I fix some dishes that are fancy and complex
With names I can hardly say aloud
And others that are easy
And are sure to please a crowd.

I've prepared recipes for the President, and for scholars;
For the famous, the rich, and for the poor
And for the lonely, and the heartbroken
Who've shown up at my door.

Even if the Ku Klux Klan came into town
Filled with hate and carrying signs

Well, I'd invite them all over for dinner
Because love conquers hate every time.

Honey, everyone gets hungry,
Everyone has to eat,
So, I'd march the Klan right to my house
And give them all a seat.

But before we could get started
They'd have to take off those sheets.
Besides, wearing a hood would just get in the way
If they're planning on getting something to eat.

I'd use my secret ingredient
To change their hearts and minds
Because praying first over a meal
Makes it taste better every time.

I've traveled around the country
And been on TV many times,
And folks near and far always claim
That they've never eaten dishes as good as mine.

They always want to know my secret,
And now I've shared it with you, too.
Pray BEFORE you start to cook
And put love into everything you do.

Introduction

et your spiritual taste buds ready because without a doubt, *Ten Ingredients for a Joyous Life and a Peaceful Home: A Spiritual Memoir* will be one of the most enticing spiritual cookbooks you've ever read! It discusses the ingredients we all need to live a blessed life. The Bible is full of ingredients needed to achieve spiritual success. The following passage outlines one set of ingredients:

> Whereby are given unto us exceeding great and precious promises: that by these ye might be partakers of the divine nature, having escaped the corruption that is in the world through lust.
>
> And beside this, giving all diligence, add to your faith virtue; and to virtue knowledge;
>
> And to knowledge temperance; and to temperance patience; and to patience godliness;
>
> And to godliness brotherly kindness; and to brotherly kindness charity. For if these things be in you, and abound, they make you that ye shall neither be barren nor unfruitful in the knowledge of our Lord Jesus Christ.
>
> But he that lacketh these things is blind, and cannot see afar off, and hath forgotten that he was purged from his old sins. Wherefore the rather, brethren, give diligence to make your calling and election sure: for if ye do these things, ye shall never fall. *2 Pet 1:4–10*

The ingredients outlined in this book are very similar to the ones described above. The ten ingredients included are the ones that have impacted Angela's life the most and can impact yours as well. Every now and then, we need someone to take us firmly by the shoulders and give us a firm shake. This book is a loving wakeup call for those of us who find ourselves sleepwalking. When we sleepwalk spiritually, we wake up to find ourselves fearful, despairing, anxious, and depressed, but we can't remember how it happened.

This book will serve as a reminder that we all need to be held accountable. Real accountability comes when you trust someone to correct and instruct you, even if you don't always understand or agree with that person. We all have a blind side—an area in our life that we're unable to see on our own and that can prove to be harmful and destructive.

Ten Ingredients for a Joyous Life and a Peaceful Home: A Spiritual Memoir serves as a spiritual mirror to reveal everything about our walk in Christ that needs to be revealed. It is written in an accessible and practical style. The depth and wealth of spiritual insights contained in each chapter makes this a landmark book that will shatter secular concepts and will rewire our thinking about our souls, ourselves, how we got to where we are today, and where we're going from here. This book will challenge you to connect the dots and see if the picture revealed resembles a worldly image of yourself or the image of Christ.

Each chapter in this book contains a Sunday School lesson. The lessons are intended to give you specific verses relevant to the ingredient discussed. I encourage you to reflect on the scriptures by yourself or discuss the lessons with others. The lessons provide a great opportunity to talk about your own experiences in Christ and how the selected verses impact your life.

We all have unique gifts that can be used for God's purpose. Anyone who is used by God to bring about His will on earth is phenomenal! I claim my apostleship along with many other gifts to include pastor and teacher. My place in the body of Christ is for the perfecting of the saints, the work of the ministry, and the edification of true holiness.

My rejoicing in Christ is this: I have experienced the mystery of godliness. God has given me a unique ability to demystify the gospel—a living document that does not grow stale with the changing times. The testimony in this book is the testimony of my conscience, given with simplicity and godly sincerity, not with fleshly wisdom. In all humility, I confess that God has given me the keys to the kingdom of Heaven. The gospel of Jesus Christ, coupled with sound doctrine, is the key that will unlock eternal life and secure you a place before the throne of God.

This is my testimony: I discovered the power of God through a simple childlike faith in Jesus Christ before I could become tainted with the institutional and conventional forms of Christianity. As a child, I never regularly attended church, although my parents did. I just didn't have an interest in church, even though I could not dismiss an uncanny fear of God. My grandfather was more discerning of my reluctance to go to church and advised my mother not to force the issue. He told my parents to leave me alone and allow God to work on me until I came around. Looking back, I'm thankful for my grandfather's wisdom.

I finished high school early and enlisted in the Army at age 17. By the time I was 18, I was married and learning to be a father to my first son. My inability or unwillingness to apply the brakes to the sin in my own life led me on a collision course that ended in divorce and a lifelong burden of guilt and collateral damage. I share with people today that a mistake is not truly a mistake if we learn something from it. The mistakes of my youth have made me a wiser and a better person.

An early exposure to the ways of sin forced me to hide my respect for and fear of God in favor of a more acceptable appearance of worldliness. Imagine a sinner being hardened by sin yet trying to respect godly bounds that he never would allow to be formally enforced. I can remember my close friend saying to me after I refused to participate in a robbery, "you just don't have the killing instinct." I quickly dismissed his remarks, but I knew that he was right.

My awareness of God encircled me like a ring of fire, clearly marking the boundaries of my actions. It's remarkable how a person can fear God to the point that it puts limits on his sinful actions, but can still know nothing about Christ and salvation. That person was me! I pacified my conscience and vowed to God that even though I wasn't ready to serve Him now, that when I did give my life to Him, I would be real and dedicated for the rest of my life. I have not gone back on that promise. Although I said that vow in secret, I honestly meant it.

Shortly thereafter, a turn of events occurred that forced me to keep my vow to God. A person I worked with did a good deed for me. When I expressed my gratitude, he took the opportunity to share his belief in Christ. My response to his testimony wasn't rude, and I admitted that I was glad for him. But I told him that I didn't see a need for Christ in my life. How we moved from me shunning this man to agreeing to talk to his pastor is still a mystery to me today! But as God would have it, I met his minister, an aged man, and he preached the gospel of Jesus Christ to me. The content of his message was simple—the death, the burial, and the resurrection of Jesus Christ.

One thing that pastor said stood out in my mind: God is greater than the devil. In the world and with the lifestyle I was living, God's greatness was not common knowledge or a proven fact. The minister also revealed, through the word of God, that Jesus Christ is the Son of God and that He sits on His right hand side. I did something that night that I had never done before. I trusted a man with my life and I opened my heart by faith to the God that I always feared but never really knew.

I remember that I released all of my pride that night. I told the Lord that I was afraid and that He would have to make an appearance to me in a special way, because if He didn't touch me, I didn't think that I could ever get back to this prayerful position again. I focused my faith on Jesus Christ sitting on the right hand side of God the Father. I asked Him to forgive me for all my sins and come into my heart. That night was the most honest I had ever allowed myself to be. The Lord delivered on His promise to save me from my sins and come into my heart. I made a profession of faith that night, August 5, 1976, around 7:30 p.m. I was 22 years old.

As a minister, I am accountable for the battle between good and evil fought daily in the conscience of mankind. This is a treacherous battleground—the casualties of war will have everlasting and eternal consequences. The stain of sin that sullies and condemns every soul can only be removed by sincere remorse and repentance toward God. The pureness of your repentance will mark the difference between simply receiving a religion and establishing a personal relationship with Jesus Christ. Righteousness, holiness, and perfection are attainable as believers in Christ. There is a practical approach to serving God. We are instructed in scripture to submit ourselves to God. If we resist the devil, he will flee.

As Christians, we are to have the mind of Christ, but what does that really mean? It simply means that we, as believers, must be taught how to allow the Bible to genuinely become our belief system. We need to be cause-driven, committed believers of moral excellence. Can you imagine how much resistance there had to be to the early doctrine of Christianity? If you read the word of God prayerfully, you will see how the Apostle Paul struggled with the ungodly, selfish Gentiles that were accustomed to immersing themselves in the perversions of that day. God has given me a ministry of reconciliation—reconciling perverted minds back to the image of Christ.

Without question, I know that even with the most valiant effort, we cannot live holy one single day without God's help. That being said, the Lord has instructed me to declare this gospel truth: by God's grace, a man, woman, boy, or girl can put their hands to the plow of salvation, trust in the power of His Holy Spirit, and never fall from their steadfastness.

Ten Ingredients for a Joyous Life and a Peaceful Home: A Spiritual Memoir is divinely ordered by God to inspire those that have fallen and encourage those that have grown weary in battle. After reading this book I expect you to be reminded of your first love: God. It should rekindle the flickering flame of your faith or relight the fire in you that started to die. The fire of godly passion must start at home before it can consume the world around us.

God is able to keep His people from falling! I encourage you to look inward and fight the good fight of faith. God gives us just what we need and just when we need it. Use this book to face your sins and shortcomings and use your faith to overcome them. Whatever God wants you to do, He will give you the power to accomplish it.

May God Bless You!

Pastor Salem Robinson, Jr.
2008

Chapter One: Love
ANGELA'S TESTIMONY

If you're like most people, you're on a search for true love. Unfortunately, most people don't realize that true love is only found when you have a loving relationship with God through His son, Jesus Christ. Once you've established that relationship, you can give love and be loved by others. But how do you do that? How do you find God? How do you accept Jesus Christ? And how do you find true love? These are ancient questions with simple answers. With the help of the Lord, I pray that you find out how to love by reading this chapter.

God loves us, but certain expectations come with His love. He has a purpose and a plan for all of us. That plan is salvation from sin through belief in the death, the burial, and the resurrection of Jesus Christ. God's love for us is manifested through Christ and our acceptance of Him as our personal savior. His love works in our lives through the Holy Spirit. It is empowered by our absolute obedience to the word of God and our desire to do the will of the Lord in our daily lives. Part of that plan is to accept Christ as your personal savior and as the mediator between man and God. Our acceptance of God's plan is how we come to know Him in truth. Accepting the truth is how we find love, from God and from others.

Now that I've become a Christian, I've finally learned how to love and be loved through the spirit of God. The thing about real love is that it is a powerful force that grows and changes you and everyone around you. Now that I know the meaning of true love, my life has never been better.

When I was about 10 years old, I realized that there is a God. For the first time, I knew that He was looking at me and at everyone in the world and although we were as small as ants, He knew each and every person individually. That day, God became a reality to me. I had an understanding, even as a child, that He existed.

I also knew that He loved me. The impact of that day has always remained with me.

My concept of love as a teenager was shaped by the times I grew up in—the 1970s. Love in the 1970s was a weird combination of secular beliefs, worldly lust, and a new interest in Christianity. Many theologians feel that the last revival to really impact the western world was the Jesus Movement in the late 60s and 70s. During the 1970s, young Christians were known as "Jesus Freaks" because of their fervent and sometimes fanatical views about religion. People were saying "I found it," but I didn't know what "it" was. Church music changed into a combination of old gospel standards and rock and roll, a fusion that became known as contemporary Christian music. There was a lot of emotion, crying, and arm waving during church services. For a short time, people talked about being born again and the power of love, love, love. It was all about love, man.

Love was a word that was used constantly by my generation without any real understanding of what it all meant. Brightly colored letters spelling LOVE were printed on t-shirts and bumper stickers, and love was portrayed in one form or another in movies, books, and songs as something romantic and involving sex. It was the free love era: if it feels good do it, love the one you're with, do it until you're satisfied. It was all very confusing for me because I didn't have a clue what "doing it" really meant. My parents constantly warned me against what others were calling fun but never explained why I needed to be careful.

I became a spectator on the sidelines of the free love movement. Deep down inside, I knew that the love I was looking for was in God, but I didn't know how to make that connection. Even as a child, I knew that serving God and being a Christian were far more powerful than what I had observed in most churches. My parents were infrequent churchgoers, but they sent me, my older sister Sandra, my brother Howard, and my baby sister Marcy to whatever church was nearest to the house. Because my father was in the Air

Force, I've attended Baptist, Methodist, Lutheran, and Catholic services as well as Protestant church services on military bases around the United States. I never heard anything during all those years of Sunday services that filled the void in my heart.

In 1974, I started college at Southwest Texas State University in San Marcos, Texas (now known as Texas State University). College is supposed to be a place where young people obtain knowledge to help prepare them for the future. Unfortunately, when most young people leave home for college they are overwhelmed by their newfound personal freedom that includes numerous opportunities for sin. I was away from home and away from any kind of parental authority for the first time. College was the gateway to any sinful thing I wanted to do.

My parents had always been fairly strict and I wasn't allowed to go out on dates very often during high school. I had just started dating during my senior year, and those occasions were few and far between. College equaled freedom—I could do what I wanted, when I wanted, and with whomever I wanted.

I was excited when I first moved into my dorm room in August 1974. I was invited to a few off campus parties where the marijuana smoke was so thick it gave me migraines. The young men I met pretended to like me, but I was looking for love and refused to have sex without it. Since they were only looking for sex, the relationships never went beyond making out, the awkward back seat grinding and groping sessions that usually marked the end of a date. I was a virgin by default—the sexual acts I didn't do physically with another person, I did in my mind. I was satisfying myself through fantasies and masturbation.

I started to compare myself to others and since I wasn't doing what my friends were doing, I wasn't that bad. I watched as my friends drank until they got sick and took drugs until they couldn't function. I could have gotten any drug I wanted, but I knew that it would only turn me into a zombie like others I'd seen who got caught up in that world. This is how the devil can deceive a person with one foot in the church and one foot in sin. I didn't know at that time that to God there aren't big sins and little sins, it's all just sin. If I had died during this sinful period of my life, I would have gone to hell for the filthy acts I committed in my conscience just as if I had committed them physically with another person.

I was morally good according to the standards of the world because I was technically a virgin, didn't drink or smoke, and went to church sometimes. I might have been deceived into thinking that I was a Christian had it not been for that day in my room when I was 10 years old. I knew that God had a higher standard that I wasn't living up to. Even though the world labeled me as virtuous, I knew I was a sinner because I sinned inwardly.

With all of the deception that surrounded me, I was still able to be honest with myself. I began to realize that there had to be more to life than what I was living and what I observed in the lives of "successful" people. I knew that there was something better and more fulfilling than what was being presented to me.

In order to remain in sin, you have to keep telling lies to yourself and everyone else around you. I'm not saying that I wasn't a liar, because I was. I lied a lot. But even as a sinner, I wanted to be told the truth and recognized it when I heard it. I wasn't hearing much truth from the young men I was dating or from the so-called friends I had in college. I wasn't finding the truth in the courses I was taking in college, or from the church services I was attending. I began to long to hear the truth.

The beautiful thing about God is that He knows the course of life of every man, woman, and child. He gives everyone on earth a chance to know Him in reality, through the acceptance of His son, Jesus Christ. My opportunity to accept Jesus Christ came in the form of the young man who was my boyfriend then, and who is my husband now, Michael Medearis.

Michael and I met in November of 1974, shortly after my 18th birthday. I was in Austin, Texas, his hometown, visiting my sister and her boyfriend. We were walking around the mall when I saw Michael for the first time. He was standing outside of a nightclub, smoking a cigarette. He looked like he couldn't decide what he wanted to do next. My sister's boyfriend knew him and introduced us. I liked him immediately. Michael worked at a nearby movie theater and told us that he could get us in for free. We were sitting in the theater when I decided that I wanted to spend more time with Michael. I was having fun being with him and I wanted to get to know him better.

After that night, Michael and I talked by phone constantly. We lived about an hour and a half from each other and had to date long distance. He came to visit me as often as he could and met my family during the Thanksgiving and the Christmas holidays. My parents liked him and we had fun. After Christmas was over, so was our budding relationship. Michael stopped calling me, so I finally called him. I wanted to know what was wrong.

Michael explained that three days after Christmas, he had accepted Jesus Christ as his personal savior. I didn't know what that meant, but I did know that his voice sounded different. He seemed peaceful and happy. I told him that I wanted to visit his church.

On Sunday, January 12, 1975, Michael drove from Austin to San Marcos to pick me up for church. I knew instantly that he wasn't the same person I'd dated before. He looked different and his conversation was all about Christ. He was still learning how to be a Christian, but he explained as much as he could about salvation and about how the Holy Spirit comes into the heart of a person when they truly repent of their sins and ask Jesus for forgiveness. He told me that he no longer smoked cigarettes or marijuana or drank alcohol, and that he no longer had a desire for them. He said that he felt at peace for the first time in his life.

We went to a small church in Austin, where I heard the gospel of Jesus Christ preached in a simple, honest way for the first time. The sermon was about how Christ came to save the world from its sins, and that He would come into your heart as a living spirit to empower you to live a Christian life. For the first time, I understood that God, through the death, the burial, and the resurrection of His Son, Jesus Christ, gives you the power to overcome sin. I realized that the Holy Spirit lives within you and that is how Christians have the power to live a life that is pleasing to God and to refrain from sin.

I felt moved to go up to the altar, and that Sunday I accepted Jesus Christ as my personal savior. Two weeks later, Michael and I got married. My family and friends were stunned, but I've always said that accepting Jesus Christ and marrying Michael were two of the best decisions I've ever made.

Accepting Christ as my personal savior was the beginning of my discovery of the meaning of true love. Each day I've spent as a Christian, I've learned more and more about what love really is. When I was young, I was caught up in the emotional side of love presented to me in books, magazines, and movies. What the secular world defines as love is almost always paired with sex. I've learned that God's love is far beyond anything that is represented in the media. God's love was evident in every aspect of my life, but I was too blind to see it until I became a Christian.

The love of God allows you the freedom to admit your imperfections and the power to overcome them so that you can love perfectly through the spirit of Christ. The love of God is the foundation of my marriage, the power that binds my family together, and a comfort to my soul.

There is power in Christianity and that power is the love of God, through His son, Jesus Christ. That powerful love shielded and protected me during my sinful years and has uplifted and strengthened me as a Christian in every aspect of my life. The beautiful thing about the love of God is that it is open to everyone who truly seeks and accepts it.

What I've learned about love is that it is pure and honest and that real love is a gift from God. It may seem strange to put love and honesty in the same sentence, but that's what true love is. God loves us and, once you become a Christian, He loves others through us. In order to be loved, you have to be honest with yourself.

If you profess to be a Christian and there is still a void in your life, or if you are feeling unloved or unlovable, it is time to honestly assess your relationship with Jesus Christ. There is transformational power in the love of God and a biblical way to tap into that power.

Comments by Pastor Salem Robinson, Jr.

Misconceptions of Love

I think the most overused and misunderstood word in the English language is "love." "I love you" ends a telephone call or text message. "I love you" is the justification for inexcusable behavior. "Do it because I love you" is the plea made for the consummation of a relationship that has been developing for no longer than a week. "I love you" is sometimes followed by the words "I hate you" from the same mouth that again finds solace in saying "I love you," creating an emotional rollercoaster ride rooted in confusion.

What does it really mean to love? Does one really have the ability to turn love on or off on a whim? Can one choose not to love? From what I hear from people who are "in love," I can safely say that love as defined and practiced by secular society is overrated. As a matter of fact, this type of love should come with a warning label, "Hazardous to your health: contains high levels of drama, lust, pain, anguish, and can lead to STDs."

"Tis better to have loved and lost than never to have loved at all," are the famous words of Alfred Lord Tennyson. This secular line of thinking can get you into a lot of trouble. If you give your heart to the Lord, you will never lose. As described below in Proverbs, Solomon gives a sobering image of the secular view of love and it's close association with sex:

> And beheld among the simple ones, I discerned among
> the youths, a young man void of understanding, Pass-
> ing through the street near her corner; and he went the
> way to her house, In the twilight, in the evening, in the
> black and dark night: And, behold, there met him a
> woman with the attire of a harlot, and subtil of heart.
> (She is loud and stubborn; her feet abide not in her

house: Now is she without, now in the streets, and lieth in wait at every corner.) So she caught him, and kissed him, and with an impudent face said unto him, I have peace offerings with me; this day have I payed my vows. Therefore came I forth to meet thee, diligently to seek thy face, and I have found thee. I have deckt my bed with coverings of tapestry, with carved works, with fine linen of Egypt. I have perfumed my bed with myrrh, aloes, and cinnamon. Come, let us take our fill of love until the morning: let us solace ourselves with loves. For the good man is not at home, he is gone a long journey. *Prov. 7:7–19*

What exactly is the true meaning of love and what does it really have to do with your life experience? First of all, God is love and there is no true love apart from the knowledge of God. The Bible says: "Thou shalt love the Lord thy God with all thy heart, and with all thy soul, and with all thy strength, and with all thy mind; and thy neighbor as thyself," (Luke 10:27). To love God is to discover life's meaning and our true purpose. When we seek to make sense of this world or find our place in it apart from a belief in God, we find ourselves chasing an elusive dream.

The secular concept of love implies that only love is needed to drive our thoughts and shape our conscience. The spiritual and biblical view of love is that God becomes the breath we take in and release with mundane effort while forming a dependency upon His existence and presence in our daily lives.

When love for God is established in us, it enables us to love others with a divine nature that is not possible on our own. Love is not secular: it is divine! Just as true forgiveness cannot be achieved without God, neither can the ability to truly love. Believe it or not, you will learn more about yourself and experience more personal growth when you extend love and good will to others.

The purpose of God bringing the Ten Commandments into

the world was to define the true meaning of love. Half of the commandments deal with man's relationship with God and the other half deals with man's relationships with others. We must first embrace God's love for us before we can extend that love to others.

The Power of Love in Action

Love is not just an emotion; it is a measurable action. In John's gospel, Jesus says, "Greater love hath no man than this, that a man lay down his life for his friends," (John 15:13). Jesus laid down His life so that we may have a chance to live. To understand the true meaning of love, we must be able to comprehend the love that God demonstrated by giving us His son as a sin offering. God's love is so great that he gave up his only son to endure the anguish of sin and the separation of death. Love is an action! We love not because we have to satisfy some feeling or selfish emotional will, but because of a steadfast will to obey God's commandments.

To love is to do what is right regardless of whether you feel like it or not. When we are instructed to love our enemies as Christians, the Lord is not telling us to become robots, but to be obedient servants to the faith.

When you love someone, you don't easily abandon him or give up on him. How dare a father abandon his children and still have the audacity to claim he loves them. When you truly love someone, you want the best for him. Jealousy cannot coexist within the heart of a person that understands and accepts the love of God. The envy that plagues others and destroys personal and professional relationships is conquered when godly love is practiced.

Have you noticed that our beliefs reflect our behavior? The ideology or philosophy that we accept will be played out in our everyday life. If we accept that God is love and that there is no love apart from God, then our hearts will act upon that truth and our lives will reap a harvest of joy and contentment.

The Biblical Definition of Happiness

In the Paul's letter to the Corinthians, "Charity suffereth long, and is kind; charity envieth not; charity vaunteth not itself, is not puffed up, Doth not behave itself unseemly, seeketh not her own, is not easily provoked, thinketh no evil; Rejoiceth not in iniquity, but rejoiceth in the truth," (1 Cor. 13:4–6). The word charity in this passage refers to love. Thus, this passage conveys the true meaning and character of love.

Love and happiness is what most people want in this life. However, their version of love is often secular love that resembles more of a condoned lust. God defines love as a divine nature that requires His involvement. It makes sense that love brings us closer to the person of God in whose image we were created.

When viewed spiritually, happiness takes on a totally different meaning as well. Happiness, as defined by God, means to be blessed. He empowers us to reach out and touch the lives of others, and by doing this, we'll enjoy a fulfillment that is described as being blessed.

Love and happiness are very much within our grasp, but can only be attained by allowing God to enlighten our minds to the true meaning of love. To those that have entered into this knowledge, when asked if you are happy, you can respond honestly: you are blessed!

As our society becomes more and more secular, God is removed from the lives and the conscience state of mankind. This denial of the existence and presence of God denies mankind of the only opportunity to experience love and happiness.

The Ten Commandments brought the knowledge of sin into the world. With that knowledge comes a way for Christians to rise beyond the ashes and ruins of a morally depraved world. When we consider the crucifixion scene where Jesus is on the cross, flanked by two other men dying similar deaths, we surmise that physical proximity to Jesus does not guarantee the security of His love. One thief wanted help without accountability while the other thief sought deliverance through salvation. The latter experienced the love of God that followed him from time to eternity. In order to receive God's love, you must do more than ask for it—you must honestly offer up your life to the Lord.

The Balance of Emotional Strength

In Ephesians 3:17–19, the Apostle Paul writes the following:

> That Christ may dwell in your hearts by faith; that ye, being rooted and grounded in love, May be able to comprehend with all saints what is the breadth, and length, and depth, and height; And to know the love of Christ, which passeth knowledge, that ye might be filled with all the fulness of God.

I love how Paul admonishes the church at Ephesus to allow the love of God to center them. That message is still relevant today and equally as urgent. God's love has to center us to help us meet the challenges that are facing us today. Christians are constantly bombarded with secular distractions designed to distance us from our faith in Christ. As believers, we must be rooted and unshakeable in our resolve to stay focused on the things that are the most important. We must stay focused on our faith and resist losing our balance.

God's love cannot be discovered or obtained intellectually. To know true love, you must surrender your will to God. Through God's omnipotent knowledge, we are informed by His word that in order to find our lives we have to first lose them: "He that findeth his life shall lose it: and he that loseth his life for my sake shall find it," (Matt. 10:39). This verse is profound. The simple message is that to find that which we lack and seek to obtain, we must look beyond ourselves.

God's Love Gives Life Meaning

To walk in love is to live a life that gives credibility to the existence of God. Living a Christian life gives meaning to an otherwise immoral and chaotic world that challenges our sanity as a human race. The love of God has everything to do with the meaning of life.

Solomon said "I have seen all the works that are done under the sun; and behold, all is vanity and vexation of spirit," (Eccles. 1:14). Solomon learned from everyday living that many things in this life don't make sense. It's our love for God and His love for us that soothes the spirit longing to make sense of the world. After we satisfy our lust, our interests, and desires, we are still empty and searching for meaning and purpose. God's love gives meaning to our existence.

Love Means Living and Speaking the Truth

When addressing the Corinthian church, the Apostle Paul resorts to irony to get his point across: "For out of much affliction and anguish of heart I wrote unto you with many tears; not that ye should be grieved, but that ye might know the love which I have more abundantly unto you," (2 Cor. 2:4). The Apostle Paul experienced the cleansing power of God's love, but has difficulty convincing others that their distorted view of what love really is can adversely affect their faith and their walk in Christ. "And I will very gladly spend and be spent for you; though the more abundantly I love you, the less I be loved," (2 Cor. 12:15). This compassionate man of God is trying to convince believers that open rebuke is better than secret love—that his love for them compels him to emphatically declare God's uncompromising truths.

Paul acknowledges that the secular view of love has impaired the Ephesian churches' ability to discern and receive the pure application of God's love. He sadly accepts that the more he loves his fellow man in God's fashion, the less they appreciate his commitment and efforts. Paul becomes aware of the sad reality that he is despised by the very people who should praise him. The prevailing view of secular love has permeated the church of God and challenges even the saints of God.

We must understand that love is not always a pat on the back, a kiss on the cheek, or even soothing words or warm accolades and praise. Love is the steadfast affirmation of truth and a constant alignment of our will with God's will. To love is to accept His truths as ours and His purpose as our purpose; to manifest our love for God by loving others as declared in His word, even when they are not being loveable. The words of Christ exhort us to love everyone with a godly love: "For if ye love them which love you, what reward have ye? do not even the publicans the same?" (Matt. 5:46).

As possessors of this divine love, we have to go beyond the bounds that limit those devoid of godly love. To love someone is to esteem their best interests, even at the expense of your own selfish gratification or self-serving needs. This is what it means to have the mind of Christ. When confronted with ambiguous decisions, we ask ourselves, "What would Jesus do?" The answer will always be that He chooses the path of love, not the path of least resistance. Sometimes, when we choose the path of love, we aren't always embraced or celebrated. But rest assured that the caress and comforting embrace from God will strengthen you to never weary in well doing.

In Jude 1:21, we are exhorted to, "Keep yourselves in the love of God, looking for the mercy of our Lord Jesus Christ unto eternal life." To love God is not only to experience an abundant life here on earth, but to also reserve hope in the life hereafter. The love of God has everything to do with who we are and what we hope to accomplish in this life and the next.

It is God's love that should shape our self-esteem. His love is the source from which we should derive our self-worth and our confidence. It should serve as our inspiration and give our lives meaning. God's love allows us to soar above the pitfalls that are devised to snare us on every side. God's love centers the very existence of who we are!

> We love him, because he first loved us. *1 John 4:19*

LOVE AND HONESTY

Truth is the foundation of Christianity and honesty is the pathway to finding real love. To love and to be loved, you have to be honest with yourself and truthful with others. Honesty, even in the house of God, is becoming a rare commodity. Honesty and truth are synonymous and are inseparable partners. The truth will set you free. To truly accept and love God, you must have an honest heart.

Honesty has more to do with your intentions and motives than to the adherence to agreed rules of conduct. Can one tell the truth and not be an honest person? Absolutely! The sad reality is that most dishonest people hide their deception behind some form of truthfulness.

The prophet Jeremiah makes one of the most profound yet misunderstood observations concerning the human heart: "The heart is deceitful above all things, and desperately wicked: who can know it?" (Jer. 17:9). The scriptures help us realize that out of the heart come the issues of life. Before sin is revealed by our actions, it must first be conceived in our thoughts and imagination.

The Psalmist says in Psalm 58:3, "The wicked are estranged from the womb, they go astray as soon as they be born, speaking lies." We have to be taught by God to be honest because we are born into this world with the innate talent to lie. Before you can effectively understand what it means to be honest, you must first understand what constitutes a lie. A person is said to be a liar when they misrepresent the truth with the intention to defraud or to deceive.

A partial truth is considered a lie when it's intended to be inconclusive in order to sway one's perception in the wrong direction. Again, most people think that you are not lying if you include some level of factual truth. But the real truth is that the greater the intensity of your effort to project a skewed image, the further you distance yourself from being defined as an honest person.

To work for God, we must have an honest report in and out of the church. As believers, we are to show honesty before God and before man. If you do all the right things, but do them for the wrong reasons, men may praise you, but you will be despised by God.

Some people think that it is honest to only give part of the truth. If you are following the conventional wisdom of "what they don't know won't hurt them," you aren't being honest. When someone is always evasive and reticent about their action or intent, it is a clear sign that they are not an honest person. Dishonest people are always leaving wiggle room in anything they commit to do.

> Now the end of the commandment is charity out of a pure heart, and of a good conscience, and of faith unfeigned. *1 Tim. 1:5*

When someone does not have a pure heart, they will succumb to the will to lie. It is remarkable in our society that honesty is no longer a valued virtue. Being honest is viewed more as a liability than an asset. Far too many people share the belief that a strategically spoken lie can serve you better than the truth. But to an honest person, lying is never an option.

When you pretend to be something that you are not because you do not possess the emotional maturity to deal with your reality, you make lies and falsehood your refuge. Just as courage is not the absence of fear, honesty is not just the absence of lies. This type of emotional weakness, the inability to face the truth about yourself, can only truly be addressed by a complete surrendering of your will and by having faith in God.

God has a way of taking someone with low self-esteem and making them giants in the faith. The facades that we've created to protect our illusions for so many years must be shattered by the gospel of Jesus Christ if we are to understand what it means to be honest.

Can you tell when someone is lying to you? The rapid or shifty eye movement may be an outward giveaway of a lie in progress, but the true formation of the lie took place long before it was ever spoken from the lips. As believers of the faith, we have been warned of the boundaries that surround every child of God. These boundaries are lovingly given by God not to restrict us but to protect us. We are commanded to abstain from the very appearance of evil—to avoid getting involved with anything that is sinful in nature and that proposes a threat to godly living.

When a Christian has an honest heart, he is not satisfied with measuring his integrity by how close he can get to the boundaries of sin without crossing the clearly marked barriers. An honest person is saddened when he entertains a course not sanctified by God. Even if ungodly persuasion entices him to step past the bounds of conscience or action, honesty quickly leads to repentance.

> For godly sorrow worketh repentance to salvation not to be repented of: but the sorrow of the world worketh death. For behold this selfsame thing, that ye sorrowed after a godly sort, what carefulness it wrought in you, yea, what clearing of yourselves, yea, what indignation, yea, what fear, yea, what vehement desire, yea, what zeal, yea, what revenge! In all things ye have approved yourselves to be clear in this matter. *2 Cor. 7:10–11*

An honest-hearted Christian regrets any failures of disobedience towards God and refuses to hide behind excuses, but openly acknowledges his sin and asks for forgiveness and guidance. Once the disappointment of failure is overshadowed by God's mercy and grace, a new person emerges with a newfound zeal to prove that his love for God is still sincere.

Honesty will clear you of sin before God, whereas dishonesty creates a quagmire in your life. Dishonest people will never know the joy of the Lord nor will they ever see the beauty in holiness. An honest spirit will give one the courage to face and conquer the things that a dishonest person will never pursue. The fear of exposing the things they dread and fear about themselves will cause dishonest people to never even consider revealing the hidden desires of the heart.

A dishonest heart will keep you emotionally immature and spiritually retarded. This is the reason why people can be so religious and yet so ungodly. They can sit in church and hear the piercing, revealing truths of the gospel demanding change and restoration, but those demands will go unheeded by the dishonest heart.

Beware of the deceit of folly! Folly is a tool of dishonesty that is used to mask true feelings. Most people who succumb to folly are generally very insecure and dishonest people. By folly, I don't mean acting jovial or being happy and perky. Personally, I know how therapeutic humor can be, but folly goes beyond light humor. Folly can become the catalyst for lies and a cloak for deceit. Be leery of people who treat everything as a joke. You have to wonder who is guarding their heart when their lips are speaking too freely. For nonbelievers, lies became their armor and truth is what they tell only when they are forced. Unfortunately, lies became so much a part of their demeanor that they fail to ever get a handle on the truth.

> Neither filthiness, nor foolish talking, nor jesting, which are not convenient: but rather giving of thanks. *Eph. 5:4*

We forget that Christianity was birthed through suffering. The first Christians were individuals who believed in the death, burial, and resurrection of Jesus Christ with genuine conviction that defined the very existence of their humanity. The immortality of the soul was honestly believed! In Satan's encounter with Job, he said that all that a man has he will give for his life. Even the devil knows that the ultimate sacrifice and proof of honest belief and commitment is when you are willing to die for what you believe in.

As modern day Christians, we too must stand next to the measuring stick of honesty and see if we stand tall enough. Keep in mind, God is not grading on a curve. Nothing has changed; Jesus Christ is the same yesterday, today, and forevermore. An honest person is changed from the inside and does not desire to do things contrary to God. Honesty is about pleasing God not only in our actions, but also with our desires, intentions, motives, and with our hearts, knowing that they are clearly seen by God. That is what it means to be honest and to truly love. Only with honesty is true, godly love possible.

PASTOR ROBINSON'S SUNDAY SCHOOL LESSON

True, godly love cannot exist without first embracing honesty. You must be honest with yourself and honest with God before you can move forward into a Christian life. The following verses will help you reflect on what it means to be honest and the role honesty should play in your life.

John 1:47–48

47 Jesus saw Nathanael coming to him, and saith of him, Behold an Israelite indeed, in whom is no guile.

48 Nathanael saith unto him, Whence knowest thou me? Jesus answered and said unto him, Before that Philip called thee, when thou wast under the fig tree, I saw thee.

Gal. 2:12–13

12 For before that certain came from James, he did eat with the Gentiles: but when they were come, he withdrew and separated himself, fearing them which were of the circumcision.

13 And the other Jews dissembled likewise with him; insomuch that Barnabas also was carried away with their dissimulation.

Rom. 12:9–19

9 Let love be without dissimulation. Abhor that which is evil; cleave to that which is good.

10 Be kindly affectioned one to another with brotherly love; in honour preferring one another;

11 Not slothful in business; fervent in spirit; serving the Lord;

12 Rejoicing in hope; patient in tribulation; continuing instant in prayer;

13 Distributing to the necessity of saints; given to hospitality.

14 Bless them which persecute you: bless, and curse not.

15 Rejoice with them that do rejoice, and weep with them that weep.

16 Be of the same mind one towards another. Mind not high things, but condescend to men of low estate. Be not wise in your own conceits.

17 Recompense to no man evil for evil. Provide things honest in the sight of all men.

18 If it be possible, as much as lieth in you, live peaceably with all men.

19 Dearly beloved, avenge not yourselves, but rather give place unto wrath: for it is written, Vengeance is mine; I will repay, saith the Lord.

Rom. 13:8–14

8 Owe no man any thing, but to love one another: for he that loveth another hath fulfilled the law.

9 For this, Thou shalt not commit adultery, Thou shalt not kill, Thou shalt not steal, Thou shalt not bear false witness, Thou shalt not covet; and if there be any other commandment, it is briefly comprehended in this saying, namely, Thou shalt love thy neighbour as thyself.

10 Love worketh no ill to his neighbour: therefore love is the fulfilling of the law.

11 And that, knowing the time, that now it is high time to awake out of sleep: for now is our salvation nearer than when we believed.

12 The night is far spent, the day is at hand: let us therefore cast off the works of darkness, and let us put on the armour of light.

13 Let us walk honestly, as in the day; not in rioting and drunkenness, not in chambering and wantonness, not in strife and envying.

14 But put ye on the Lord Jesus Christ, and make not provision for the flesh, to fulfil the lusts thereof.

2 Cor. 4:1–2

1 Therefore seeing we have this ministry, as we have received mercy, we faint not;

2 But have renounced the hidden things of dishonesty, not walking in craftiness, nor handling the word of God deceitfully; but by manifestation of the truth commending ourselves to every man's conscience in the sight of God.

Luke 8:11–15

11 Now the parable is this: The seed is the word of God.

12 Those by the way side are they that hear; then cometh the devil, and taketh away the word out of their hearts, lest they should believe and be saved.

13 They on the rock are they, which, when they hear, receive the word with joy; and these have no root, which for a while believe, and in time of temptation fall away.

14 And that which fell among thorns are they, which, when they have heard, go forth, and are choked with cares and riches and pleasures of this life, and bring no fruit to perfection.

15 But that on the good ground are they, which in an honest and good heart, having heard the word, keep it, and bring forth fruit with patience.

Acts 6:1–4

1 And in those days, when the number of the disciples was multiplied, there arose a murmuring of the Grecians against the Hebrews, because their widows were neglected in the daily ministration.

2 Then the twelve called the multitude of the disciples unto them, and said, It is not reason that we should leave the word of God, and serve tables.

3 Wherefore, brethren, look ye out among you seven men of honest report, full of the Holy Ghost and wisdom, whom we may appoint over this business.

4 But we will give ourselves continually to prayer, and to the ministry of the word.

Phil. 4:6–9

6 Be careful for nothing; but in every thing by prayer and supplication with thanksgiving let your requests be made known unto God.

7 And the peace of God, which passeth all understanding, shall keep your hearts and minds through Christ Jesus.

8 Finally, brethren, whatsoever things are true, whatsoever things are honest, whatsoever things are just, whatsoever things are pure, whatsoever things are lovely, whatsoever things are of good report; if there be any virtue, and if there be any praise, think on these things.

9 Those things, which ye have both learned, and received, and heard, and seen in me, do: and the God of peace shall be with you.

1 Pet. 2:11–12

11 Dearly beloved, I beseech you as strangers and pilgrims, abstain from fleshly lusts, which war against the soul;

12 Having your conversation honest among the Gentiles: that, whereas they speak against you as evildoers, they may by your good works, which they shall behold, glorify God in the day of visitation.

1 Tim. 2:1–2

1 I exhort therefore, that, first of all, supplications, prayers, intercessions, and giving of thanks, be made for all men;

2 For kings, and for all that are in authority; that we may lead a quiet and peaceable life in all godliness and honesty.

Heb. 13:17–18

17 Obey them that have the rule over you, and submit yourselves: for they watch for your souls, as they that must give account, that they may do it with joy, and not with grief: for that is unprofitable for you.

18 Pray for us: for we trust we have a good conscience, in all things willing to live honestly.

Rom. 1:18

18 For the wrath of God is revealed from heaven against all ungodliness and unrighteousness of men, who hold the truth in unrighteousness.

LOVE

SIS. ESSI EARGLE

Love is begotten of God and our Lord and Savior Jesus Christ. Without God and Christ in your life, love is inconceivable. God and Christ in your life through salvation is the beginning of the understanding of true love.

Love is unconditional. It resides in the heart; it cannot be turned off. Love will not lie but will be truthful even when it hurts. With that foundation, I shall attempt to graze the surface with imagery of love as a servant of our Lord and Savior Jesus Christ, Son of the true and living God, the epitome of incomprehensible love.

Love is as smooth as satin being carried by the wind. It is as deep as oceans of royal purple. It is as soothing as the sun warming the skin of your back on a cold day.

Love is as beautiful as a diamond, surprising the eyes with a glimmer of many colors. It is as elegant as a rose, without wither, in full bloom.

Love is as sweet as a ripe honeydew melon in the morning followed by actions that express 'I love you' without words.

Love is as graceful as the spread of a peacock's feathers in courtship for a mate.

Love is as hypnotic as piano keys played in an enchanting melody. Love is as beautiful as a full moon mirroring the reflection of the sun. Love is in the open, not secret.

As the King James Bible in Corinthians describes, in these things doth love abide:

> Charity suffereth long, and is kind, charity envieth not; charity vaunteth not itself, is not puffed up, doth not behave itself unseemly, seeketh not her own, is not easily provoked, thinketh no evil; Rejoiceth not in

iniquity, but rejoiceth in truth; Beareth all things, believeth all things, hopeth all things, endureth all things. *1 Cor. 13:4–8*

Love never fails. "And now abideth faith, hope, charity, these three; but the greatest of these is charity," (1 Cor. 13:13).

Chapter Two: Forgiveness
ANGELA'S TESTIMONY

I've learned that there is power in Christianity. With the help of the Lord, I have the ability to do things that would have been unimaginable before I became a Christian. I've learned that forgiveness is a divine gift, whether it is the forgiveness of our sins through the blood of Jesus Christ, the power we're given as Christians to forgive others, or the ability we possess through the spirit of Christ to forgive ourselves.

My struggles with the Christian concepts of forgiveness weren't because I held ill feelings against others. I've never been one to hold a grudge. It's the inability to forgive myself for the things I've done and the mistakes that I've made that causes me to struggle. My big mouth has certainly gotten me into a lot of trouble! I've had to learn how to forgive myself when I've ignorantly said or done something hurtful. I realize that I've often acted in an inconsiderate way because I didn't consider the feelings of others first. I've had to learn to admit that I was at fault, and to ask for forgiveness and the power to overcome my transgression. These lessons have been essential to my growth as a Christian.

The ability to ask for forgiveness for your sins is one of the first steps in becoming a Christian. Pride often prevents us from seeking forgiveness. After you repent of your sins against God and others, peace will fill your soul. In order to be forgiven, you must humble yourself and ask for forgiveness. It's the asking that seems to be the hard part for most folks like me. It's human nature not to want to admit that you've been wrong.

I've found that when you truly repent from your heart and honestly want to be forgiven for your transgressions, you'll receive the power from the Holy Spirit that will enable you to overcome the offense and to keep you from repeating it again. That's the sign of true repentance—you don't make that mistake again. That's also how you know that the Holy Spirit is working in your life and that you've truly repented of your sins—you never return to those sins again.

The divine ability to forgive is what provides harmony in our relationships. Part of the reason for numerous divorces in our society is a direct result of the inability of the husband, the wife, or both parties to forgive and move forward. Anger, hurt, and misunderstandings will eat away at the foundation of a marriage like acid if no forgiveness is present.

I'm always saddened when I hear about family members or former friends that have stopped speaking to each other because of a misunderstanding. It takes a lot of time, energy, and anger to keep a disagreement fueled for years. What a waste! There's no way that you can call yourself a Christian with that kind of anger and bitterness in your heart. There is a freedom in forgiveness that can only be experienced if you have the courage to humble yourself and ask for it. If you haven't tapped into the divine power of forgiveness, I urge you to prayerfully seek it out today.

Death and judgment day await us all, so while you have the time and the ability to repent, and the mercy of God is upon you, humble your heart and do it. Don't fall into the trap of deciding what God will or will not forgive. Don't decide if a person will forgive you before seeking their forgiveness. Extend the same forgiveness to yourself that God has showered down upon all of us. Ask for forgiveness from a repentant heart and let the working power of the Holy Spirit intercede on your behalf.

Everyday, I try to prayerfully focus on the things I need to purify in my heart and my conscience and ask for forgiveness and the strength to overcome my failings. The Lord has given me the grace to overcome the outward sins and weaknesses that every Christian should be free from the moment they make a confession of faith and repent of their sins. He has also given me the grace and the faith to resist the temptations that Satan dangles in front of every Christian to lure them back into the world of sin—the lust of the flesh, the lust of the eye, and pride. The Lord gives His people a spirit of discernment to recognize these worldly temptations, even when they're all wrapped up in a pretty package and seem harmless.

I've turned down a number of seemingly fabulous opportunities because I knew that underneath all the glitter, a snare set by Satan that would put my soul in jeopardy. It's the personal faults and shortcomings that I ask for forgiveness to overcome. Sometimes, I'm not as patient as I should be, or I might have said something hurtful. Maybe I wasn't as considerate as I could have been—the list goes on and on. I have to forgive myself when I fail, learn from it, and pray for the Lord to forgive me, ask for forgiveness from the person I've offended, and move forward.

Even though I know that I have a long way to go as a Christian, the forgiveness that Christ extended to me through His death on the cross and the triumphs I've made each day on this Christian journey give me the courage to continue. When I think about the forgiveness I've received from God and from those whom I've offended over the years, it makes it easy for me to extend that same love and forgiveness to others when they offend me.

Whether you're asking for forgiveness from God through His son, Jesus Christ, you need to repent to someone with whom you've had a disagreement, or if you need to forgive yourself, take this opportunity to make the choice to forgive. Have the courage through Jesus Christ to free yourself from the burdens you've been carrying for so long. Seeking forgiveness is one of the first steps to finding true joy and peace in your life. I pray that you find freedom through the power of divine forgiveness.

Comments by Pastor Salem Robinson, Jr.

To understand forgiveness we must view it from the peak of Christianity rather than from the valley of despair. Unbeknownst to many, true forgiveness can only be accomplished by godly intervention. You see, forgiveness is not human: it is divine.

Forgiveness: The Key to Harmony

Forgiveness is a household word, even in homes that don't believe in God. I know that we love to use the term forgiveness when instructing someone to not hold a grudge or to relinquish any ill feelings toward another. Again, the truth is that there is no such thing as being able to forgive someone without the empowerment of God. Just as marriage is designed to be between a man and a woman who fear and believe in God, so was forgiveness designed for submissive believers of the faith in order to purge divisions in the body of Christ.

> That there should be no schism in the body; but that the members should have the same care one for another. *1 Cor. 12:25*

Forgiveness is ordained by God for the purpose of maintaining love and harmony between God's people. It is the willful act of beholding one another through the eyes of mercy and compassion. There is no way that a heart that has not experienced the awakening of grace and mercy can even fathom winning the battle over entrenched hatred, bitterness, and resentment. Without God, our futile, misguided efforts at forgiveness may not have a visible presence but there is damage raging beneath.

To understand forgiveness, we must realize that it is natural to feel anger towards the person we need to forgive. Forgiveness does not come easy for most people, as this verse from Proverbs illustrates: "A brother offended is harder to be won than a strong city: and their contentions are like the bars of a castle," (Prov. 18:19).

Our human instinct is to go into self-protection mode when we've been injured or offended. Even Christians don't just naturally overflow with mercy and forgiveness when we've been wronged. We must learn to forgive through Christ.

Forgiveness is a conscious choice and can be characterized as a physical act involving our will being surrendered in obedience to a higher purpose. I believe forgiveness is a choice we make of our own will, motivated by obedience to God's command to forgive.

Saying "I forgive you" as part of social etiquette in response to someone's inexcusable behavior is not even remotely reflective of true forgiveness. Think of something truly wicked that has been done to you or to someone you love, not by accident or in error, but deliberately and with malice. Did you honestly address your feelings with a godly perspective of forgiveness or did you handle it with your own judgment and emotions?

FORGIVE AND FORGET?

The inability to truly forgive is often due to a false concept that forgetting is forgiving. Forgetting is NOT forgiving—it is a state of denial. Forgetting acts that inflicted pain is not a prerequisite to forgiveness. However, forgetting, in the sense that the act is not absent from your memory but simply not hindering your forward movement, is necessary to forgiveness. You will never have a future when you're stuck in the past. Again, forgiveness is divine.

> Brethren, I count not myself to have apprehended: but this one thing I do, forgetting those things which are behind, and reaching forth unto those things which are before. *Phil. 3:13*

Would you believe that God requires our permission to wipe away our guilt? You must choose to forgive yourself if you want to experience God's cleansing power. God is not knocking down doors to get to you; it is your choice to open the door to your heart and let Him in.

> Behold, I stand at the door, and knock: if any man hear my voice, and open the door, I will come in to him, and will sup with him, and he with me. *Rev. 3:20*

LOVING THE UNLOVEABLE

As believers we are commanded to love even when someone is not being lovable. Likewise, we are also commanded to forgive even if we feel that someone is undeserving of our forgiveness. Remember, forgiveness is never complete until, first, we have experienced the forgiveness of God, second, we can forgive others who have wronged us, and third, we are able to forgive ourselves.

Even after becoming Christians, if we want to continue to receive forgiveness from God, we must be willing to forgive others their trespasses against us. Do you know someone who despises you or loves to toy with your emotions? You should never allow those people to hold you hostage by not allowing youself to forgive them. By not forgiving them, you embolden your enemy's manipulation over your emotions by becoming a puppet on a string, helpless and unable to sever the strings that control you.

In the following verse, Moses gives a perfect illustration of forgiveness concerning someone that is your enemy: "If thou meet thine enemy's ox or his ass going astray, thou shalt surely bring it back to him again. If thou see the ass of him that hateth thee lying under his burden, and wouldest forbear to help him, thou shalt surely help with him," (Ex. 23:4–5). Look at this man seeing his enemy's ox and ass needing help. He did what was commanded of him without the interference of his emotions. When you forgive someone, you exonerate your own heart before God, but there is nothing you can do about the disposition of the heart of your enemy. Forgiveness has more to do with your heart before God than it does with the person you are forgiving.

> So likewise shall my heavenly Father do also unto you, if ye from your hearts forgive not every one his brother their trespasses. *Matt. 18:35*

It becomes apparent that you know you have a forgiving heart when you can obey God by doing what you know is right regardless of the feelings of your enemy:

> But I say unto you, Love your enemies, bless them that curse you, do good to them that hate you, and pray for them which despitefully use you, and persecute you; That ye may be the children of your Father which is in heaven: for he maketh his sun to rise on the evil and on the good, and sendeth rain on the just and on the unjust. *Matt. 5:44–45*

Love is more about our actions than an emotional state of wellbeing. Forgiveness is a course of action that is chosen in order to better align your purpose in life with God's purpose. God cannot use you in building His kingdom on earth if your heart is defiled with hatred or resentment. Forgiveness is about washing your heart from these agents of sin in order to become a clean vessel ready for God's use.

How do you forgive those who have not received forgiveness before God because of their blatant rebellion and rejection of His truths? Are you really expected to forgive their barrage of impenitent cruel offenses even though repentance is nowhere to be found in them? The answer is yes! Again, you have not been freed from your obligation to love others just because they do not love God or you.

ACHIEVING EMOTIONAL STABILITY THROUGH FORGIVENESS

We do not live in a perfect world and we get hurt, not just physically but also emotionally and spiritually. Life is tough and Satan doesn't play fair! We get discouraged, depressed, and disappointed. We experience failure, fatigue, frustration, and fears. We all carry hidden hurts from our past and we also carry wounds, battle scars, and emotional baggage. The good news is that God wants to heal our emotions and restore our souls.

Many of the emotional problems we experience are caused by a sinful life. These negative experiences leave us with unhealthy emotional complexes that take part in shaping our personalities. We hide our real selves with fake facades and resort to ego-protecting defense mechanisms to justify unrighteous behavior.

Forgiveness is a powerful tool that helps new Christians realize their potential. The question then is this—is emotional stability synonymous with spiritual conversion? With the new birth, are emotional complexes, fake facades, defense mechanisms, and all of the problems of our sinful lives that shaped our personalities resolved? Once we get saved, is this emotional, spiritual newborn baby suddenly made stable through this spiritual experience?

Nicodemus asked Jesus an historical question, "How can a man be born when he is old, can he enter the second time into his mother's womb, and be born?" (John 3:4). The new birth is still as much a mystery today as it was when Jesus enlightened Nicodemus. True believers can attest that all their worries, fears, and despondences do not instantly disappear upon a profession of faith and an acceptance of the Holy Spirit. Even though the Christian journey begins with a sincere repentance, we have to constantly focus on our new selves created in righteousness. This is why it is so important to seek out a bible teaching/believing church when professing a hope in Christ. Scripture and forgiveness can help you through the adjustment period.

In the following passage, the Apostle Paul is saying that his job as a pastor is to challenge other's faith with the truth of the gospel and empower them to address those sins of the heart: "For what thanks can we render to God again for you, for all the joy wherewith we joy for your sakes before our God; Night and day praying exceedingly that we might see your face, and might perfect that which is lacking in your faith?" (1 Thess. 3:9–10).

This is the same revelation of truth that the Apostle James was referring to when he said: "Wherefore lay apart all filthiness and superfluity of naughtiness, and receive with meekness the engrafted word, which is able to save your souls. But be ye doers of the word, and not hearers only, deceiving your own selves," (James 1:21–22).

The mystery of Christianity is revealed from heaven to those truth seekers who are willing to surrender their will to an unseen God. Emotional and spiritual stability and maturity starts and ends with a heart willing to judge ourselves daily and use our faith to put away those contrary sins.

Grudges develop when we hold on to the emotional or physical pain that other people have inflicted on us. We get mad at them and we won't let go of the anger. The person may not have even planned to intentionally hurt us, but we got hurt just the same. Our emotional pain causes us to develop a grudge, and we won't let it go. These are damaged emotions. As Christians, we must learn to give up grudges.

The Bible says, "For wrath killeth the foolish man, and envy slayeth the silly one," (Job 5:2). Why is this so? Because wrath, revenge, and envy are all self destructive—they hurt you! They cause broken relationships and will hinder emotional wounds from healing. The reason you hold a grudge is because of something in your past. Your past is past; it does not need to last a lifetime. Your past can't hurt you today unless you keep allowing it to do so. The person who hurt you may not even be alive. They may have died years ago, yet you are still holding a grudge. Think about it, they're still hurting you from the grave because you won't let it go.

Allow your faith to take precedence over your emotions and heed these words: "And forgive us our debts, As we forgive our debtors," (Matt. 6:12).

The Power of Forgiveness

As we've seen, forgiveness does not mean that you are free from having a vexation of spirit. We are told that being angry is not a sin but what we do when we are angry can lead to sin. Forgiveness is the power that allows us to "let go and let God."

> Take heed to yourselves: If thy brother trespass against thee, rebuke him; and if he repent, forgive him. And if he trespass against thee seven times in a day, and seven times in a day turn again to thee, saying, I repent; thou shalt forgive him. And the apostles said unto the Lord, Increase our faith. *Luke 17:3–5*

Jesus explained to his disciples about the mandatory requirement to love and forgive even when the violations and sins against them reached epidemic proportions. Being overwhelmed with what they perceived as an unrealistic expectation, they cried out to Jesus, "Lord, increase our faith!" The carnal mind cannot digest this type of spiritual forgiveness.

Repentance and Forgiveness

The church has an obligation to keep its members in line with scriptures of forgiveness. The passage below outlines this belief:

> Sufficient to such a man is this punishment, which was inflicted of many. So that contrariwise ye ought rather to forgive him, and comfort him, lest perhaps such a one should be swallowed up with overmuch sorrow. Wherefore I beseech you that ye would confirm your love toward him. For to this end also did I write, that I might know the proof of you, whether ye be obedient in all things. To whom ye forgive any thing, I forgive also: for if I forgave any thing, to whom I forgave it, for your sakes forgave I it in the

person of Christ; Lest Satan should get an advantage of us: for we are not ignorant of his devices. *2 Cor. 2:6–11*

Paul explains to the church that when someone walks in disobedience to God, the congregation of the church has an obligation to make that person feel uncomfortable in their mist. When the transgressor feels unaccepted, he is forced to deal with the sins within his own conscience. Once the transgressor is convicted by God and willing to turn and repent, the church has an obligation to forgive and console that person. Paul concludes that forgiveness is necessary for spiritual and emotional restoration. He warns that to forget this would be playing right into the hands of Satan.

Jesus Christ is the embodiment of God's compassion. When he cried on the cross, "Father forgive them..." the spiritual liberation that was unleashed through forgiveness was immeasurable. Unfortunately, God does not forgive us until we repent and admit our wrongdoings. In Acts 2:38, Peter commanded the people that had delivered Christ to death that they should repent before they would be forgiven. Repentance means that you become godly sorrowful of your transgressions and then ask God for forgiveness.

Forgiveness towards others must be a direct reflection of God's forgiveness toward you. If you model your forgiveness toward others with an awareness of Christ's forgiveness to you, the power of forgiveness becomes a reality.

PASTOR ROBINSON'S SUNDAY SCHOOL LESSON

FORGIVENESS AND BITTERNESS

Bitterness is unresolved anger that results in feelings of resentment. If you ever want to move from the past to the future, you must learn to just let some things go. Bitterness is the direct result of not letting forgiveness into your life. Meditate on the following verses when you need to let go of bitterness and welcome forgiveness.

Acts 8:9–24

9 But there was a certain man, called Simon, which beforetime in the same city used sorcery, and bewitched the people of Samaria, giving out that himself was some great one:

10 To whom they all gave heed, from the least to the greatest, saying, This man is the great power of God.

11 And to him they had regard, because that of long time he had bewitched them with sorceries.

12 But when they believed Philip preaching the things concerning the kingdom of God, and the name of Jesus Christ, they were baptized, both men and women.

13 Then Simon himself believed also: and when he was baptized, he continued with Philip, and wondered, beholding the miracles and signs which were done.

14 Now when the apostles which were at Jerusalem heard that Samaria had received the word of God, they sent unto them Peter and John:

15 Who, when they were come down, prayed for them, that they might receive the Holy Ghost:

16 (For as yet he was fallen upon none of them: only they were baptized in the name of the Lord Jesus.)

17 Then laid they their hands on them, and they received the Holy Ghost.

18 And when Simon saw that through laying on of the apostles' hands the Holy Ghost was given, he offered them money,

19 Saying, Give me also this power, that on whomsoever I lay hands, he may receive the Holy Ghost.

20 But Peter said unto him, Thy money perish with thee, because thou hast thought that the gift of God may be purchased with money.

21 Thou hast neither part nor lot in this matter: for thy heart is not right in the sight of God.

22 Repent therefore of this thy wickedness, and pray God, if perhaps the thought of thine heart may be forgiven thee.

23 For I perceive that thou art in the gall of bitterness, and in the bond of iniquity.

24 Then answered Simon, and said, Pray ye to the Lord for me, that none of these things which ye have spoken come upon me.

Eph. 4:31–32

31 Let all bitterness, and wrath, and anger, and clamour, and evil speaking, be put away from you, with all malice:

32 And be ye kind one to another, tenderhearted, forgiving one another, even as God for Christ's sake hath forgiven you.

Heb. 12:14–15

14 Follow peace with all men, and holiness, without which no man shall see the Lord:

15 Looking diligently lest any man fail of the grace of God; lest

any root of bitterness springing up trouble you, and thereby many be defiled.

James 3:10–16

10 Out of the same mouth proceedeth blessing and cursing. My brethren, these things ought not so to be.

11 Doth a fountain send forth at the same place sweet water and bitter?

12 Can the fig tree, my brethren, bear olive berries? either a vine, figs? so can no fountain both yield salt water and fresh.

13 Who is a wise man and endued with knowledge among you? let him shew out of a good conversation his works with meekness of wisdom.

14 But if ye have bitter envying and strife in your hearts, glory not, and lie not against the truth.

15 This wisdom descendeth not from above, but is earthly, sensual, devilish.

16 For where envying and strife is, there is confusion and every evil work.

Col. 3:19–21

19 Husbands, love your wives, and be not bitter against them.

20 Children, obey your parents in all things: for this is well pleasing unto the Lord.

21 Fathers, provoke not your children to anger, lest they be discouraged.

Acts 15:36–41

36 And some days after Paul said unto Barnabas, Let us go again and visit our brethren in every city where we have preached the word of the Lord, and see how they do.

37 And Barnabas determined to take with them John, whose surname was Mark.

38 But Paul thought not good to take him with them, who departed from them from Pamphylia, and went not with them to the work.

39 And the contention was so sharp between them, that they departed asunder one from the other: and so Barnabas took Mark, and sailed unto Cyprus;

40 And Paul chose Silas, and departed, being recommended by the brethren unto the grace of God.

41 And he went through Syria and Cilicia, confirming the churches.

Chapter Three: Service
Angela's Testimony

s a young Christian, I was taught about the importance of serving the Lord. Evidently, I didn't know the meaning of the word "serve." For years, I lived my Christian life as if the Lord was supposed to serve me. As a matter of fact, my early walk in Christ was all about me. I might do a few things here and there to make it seem like I was a loving and giving Christian, but in reality, I was always looking for the payoff. I may not have admitted that my service to the Lord was in the hopes that I'd get a blessing, but that was my underlying motivation. Most of the "service" I did then was directly related to how I would look in the eyes of others. This is the definition of hypocrisy.

Somehow, along my journey as a Christian, I had strayed from the biblical truths of serving the Lord out of a pure heart with gladness and gratitude for all that He had done for me. Most importantly, I had forgotten all about the importance of living (not just talking about) the biblical truths of Christianity. I became caught up in a prosperity-driven mindset that promotes the theory that what you do for the Lord is reflected by "blessings" in the form of your bank account, the amount of your worldly goods, and your career.

The religion of prosperity dictates the square footage of your house, the kind of cars you drive, and the clothes you wear: wealth becomes a direct indicator of your status with God. While being poor is neither a requirement nor a guarantee that you're going to heaven, being prosperous isn't an indicator of the condition of your heart before God nor is it an indication of God's blessing. What I didn't realize then is that Satan finds ways to provide you with worldly goods that blind you to the word of God, tempt you, and lead you astray. The lure of money and the pleasures of this world will entice a weak Christian, and that is what I had become. My life was a walking contradiction because I wanted to have one foot in the church and the other in the world. I wasn't fully committed to Christ, but I didn't want the stigma of being a sinner.

I was so busy running my life in my own way that I had totally left God out of the picture. I was self-directed and self-absorbed. Everything was about me and what I wanted. I really didn't know Christ in a personal way. This is a big problem if you claim that you love God and you're a Christian!

Because of my disobedience to the will and word of God, my life as a Christian was loveless, filled with turmoil, and hypocritical for years. As I write this, I realize that many people will think that I was drinking, doing drugs, having an affair, or any number of other sinful things. However, I was not going through any of that type of drama. My unhappiness was because I had obtained everything in life that was supposed to make you happy, and yet, something was still missing.

If you were on the outside looking in, my life then looked almost perfect. I was married to a kind and caring man: we had a beautiful family, successful careers, a lovely home and nice cars, beautiful clothes, and all the other material things that we've been taught are indicators of a successful life. We went to church every Sunday, and we said that we were Christians, so why did I feel so unfulfilled?

I already had all of the things that the world says you need to be happy. I even met the standard that most modern churches say are direct evidence of "God blessing you." What I didn't have then that I have now is the heavenly joy that is God given and unwavering no matter what life may bring, the peace that only comes from being a part of the will of God, and a personal relationship with Jesus Christ. I was missing these important ingredients in my life and I began to search for a way to obtain them.

I was tired of playing the role of a hypocrite with all the outward trappings of success. About ten years ago, I started attending a church led by Pastor Salem Robinson, Jr., where the gospel of

Jesus Christ is preached according to the word of God; not Pastor Robinson's opinions. As I listened to him teach and preach on Wednesdays and Sundays, my conscience, which I had conveniently been ignoring for years, awakened. My ears opened up to the truth that he was preaching. I realized that I wasn't obedient to God and that I had never established a personal relationship with Christ, even though I claimed that He had saved me from my sins.

Although I accepted Christ before my marriage, I never made the full commitment that every Christian needs to make. I hadn't studied or embraced the word of God in a way that would allow me to establish a personal relationship with Christ. As I reflect back on that time, it wasn't so much that I was outwardly doing things that were a sin against God. The inner workings of my heart and conscience were being judged by God. I was a hypocrite.

I wasted a lot of precious time that I could have been using to serve the Lord to create numerous weak and self-righteous excuses about why I was a hypocrite. I told myself that only my pastor could really live the way that we were being taught, and that I was focused on my career and making money so that I could help support the work of the Lord. I used to deceive myself into thinking I was serving the Lord and living a Christian life because I was doing most of what was right. I spent a lot of time and energy finding ways to justify my lack of obedience, looking for loopholes in the scriptures (there aren't any, trust me, I've checked), comparing myself to others, and then patting myself on the back because I thought I was living my life a little better than they were living theirs. These are the classic signs of hypocrisy—the Bible is full of examples of this lack of faith and vividly details the end of those who claim that they are Christians while living in this sin.

There isn't anything difficult or hard about Christianity or serving the Lord once you make up your mind and settle in your heart to make a full and honest commitment to Him. I was making my Christian journey difficult because I didn't want to do everything

I knew that I should be doing. I wanted to do things my way, not God's way. I wanted to implement my plan for my life and have God bless me anyway. My struggles to fully surrender my life to Christ were an inner rebellion and a war of the conscience. I finally realized that I couldn't serve the Lord until I cleaned up my conscience and made up my mind to be totally obedient to the word of God.

There was no one but myself to blame for the condition of my Christian life. I made the choice to be deceitful and to be disobedient. It was my own fault that I didn't feel the peace and joy that I observed in other Christians. My pastor taught the word of God perfectly by percept and example, but I refused to do it. Pastor Robinson teaches and preaches from the Bible and believes that as a minister, he should set the example of how a Christian should live. I can't stress enough how important it is to have a minister who has made a 100% commitment to Christ as the head of the church you attend, and yes, you need a church to attend.

God used Pastor Robinson to try to give me a message about my lack of commitment to Christ through his sermons and Sunday School lessons. I saw my failure to live a Christian life in black and white on the printed pages of the Bible week after week for years. Instead of going to the Lord in prayer and asking Pastor Robinson to counsel me so I could quit pretending, I just kept on with the little drama I was presenting to the world day in and day out. I had the word of God and living examples of how to serve the Lord before me. The Lord had left me without an excuse. I had to accept the fact that my failures in life were of my own making and take responsibility to make the changes I needed to make.

The Lord deserved far more from me than the small amount of time I was giving Him on an occasional Wednesday night or Sunday morning or when I did a little volunteer service for the church. It wasn't until I learned how to have a personal relationship with Christ that my life truly changed.

The keys to a personal relationship with Jesus Christ are an absolute surrender of your will, an honest repentance of your sins, and a desire to do the will of the Lord by applying the word of God to your life. This way you can live what you've learned each day through the power of the Holy Spirit with a clean conscience and a pure and honest heart. I've come to learn that every Christian's daily task is to love yourself and others perfectly so that you can see Him in peace when you die. There is a heaven and there is a hell and God, through His Son, Jesus Christ provides you with the opportunity in this life to chose where you want to spend eternity.

I was a Christian for more than 30 years before I ever prayerfully asked the Lord "what do you want me to do?" That simple question changed my life, because He answered me through the word of God and the sermons I heard. It began to seem like Pastor Robinson was preaching to me! The Sunday School lessons answered the questions I had about my Christian life. Most importantly, I began to listen and understand the word of God. I became obedient to His will for my life for first time. Prayer works just like a meaningful conversation, you have to ask the right questions and listen for the answers. Once I learned how to pray, I learned how to love and how to be loved, and how to serve the Lord willingly and from a pure heart. It all began with my commitment to do the will of the Lord daily, not just pay lip service to Christianity.

I took the focus off of myself and what I thought I wanted from the Lord and realized that as a Christian, this life isn't about me. I began studying the word of God and living my life honestly with a clean conscience. I realized that as a Christian, I am a walking testimony of the miraculous working power of the Holy Spirit and that my daily life should reflect that. I also began to share my testimony publicly with others whenever I had the opportunity. I've learned that it's our duty as Christians not only to live an exemplary life, but also to share our faith with others as we're led by the spirit of God.

My writing abilities are God given, but I wasn't using them for His glory, I was using them for my own. I've been blessed to write and publish 95 children's books and five cookbooks. I worked for more than 20 years of my Christian life as an author, sometimes 7 days a week, totally focused on my career. My determination to succeed in the publishing world didn't leave much time for the Lord.

The thing about Jesus that is so wonderful is that He looks at your heart and bears with you knowing that if you sincerely want to serve Him, there will come a time when you'll realize that 50% won't do, you have to make a full commitment to Christ. I was a 50 percenter for years (okay, sometimes 25%, sometimes 10%), until I realized that after all the Lord had done for me, I needed to give my all for Him.

After a long struggle and a lot of prayer, I made a complete spiritual, personal, and career change. I made a full commitment to everything, including my marriage, my family, and my new career in television. My husband and I entered by faith into the field of multimedia production. Our new business is uncharted territory for us, but the Lord knows all things. Together, we've learned how to lean and depend on faith and prayers to navigate through the dark times and how to give the Lord His rightful glory when He brings us out into the light. Although I never dreamed I would be doing a television cooking show and writing about food and culinary history, it has become my passion.

I didn't understand the direction the Lord was leading me in until I realized that food is a universal way to reach all people. Television has allowed me to bring my testimony to the masses. I also write more now than I ever have before because I do all the scripts and research for our productions, write newspaper and magazine articles, and write cookbooks. My new commitment to Christ led me to write this book, something I never even considered doing a few years ago.

Being taught the word of God, studying, praying, living a life of faith, and doing what the Lord wants me to do have filled my life with blessings I never imagined possible. All the material things I had didn't make me happy. It has been the intangible blessings I've received that have given me the joy and peace I was looking for. The spiritual blessings I've received from God have spilled over to my family and to everyone I meet. Every part of my life is better in every way. I pray that you find the same peace and contentment that I've been blessed with since I've learned how to truly serve the Lord.

COMMENTS BY PASTOR SALEM ROBINSON, JR.

HUMILITY, SELF-DENIAL, AND SERVICE

 Serving the Lord is much like having a lengthy and prosperous marriage—both must be done one day at a time!

Serving the Lord with all humility of mind, and with many tears, and temptations, which befell me by the lying in wait of the Jews: And how I kept back nothing that was profitable unto you, but have shewed you, and have taught you publickly, and from house to house, testifying both to the Jews, and also to the Greeks, repentance toward God, and faith toward our Lord Jesus Christ. *Acts 20:19–21*

Humility is the prerequisite to being honored before God, and is a state of mind. It is a constant state of self-denial, allowing the word of God to have control over your will. Just like a tree that must bear roots downward before it can bear fruit upward, you must lose sight of your own selfishness before you can expect to grow tall in the Lord.

God's servant Paul lived an exemplary life before believers and nonbelievers, both Jews and Greeks. He was able to say, "Be ye followers of me even as I also am of Christ," (1 Cor. 11:1). The reason why most professed Christians are so slothful in their service to the Lord today is because the promise of an eternal reward has not become their reality. They cannot think or perceive past their earthly lives, therefore they relinquish their hold on the hope of heaven and grasp after the rudiments of the world. Remember this verse: "If ye then be risen with Christ, seek those things which are above, where Christ sitteth on the right hand of God. Set your affection on things above, not on things on the earth. For ye are dead, and your life is hid with Christ in God," (Col. 3:1–3).

The Apostle Paul is one of the heroes of the Bible. His life paints a clear picture of what it takes to serve the Lord. In serving the Lord, the first guiding principle is to realize that it's not about you. However, the concept of our lives being hidden or suppressed in order for Christ to take center stage is easier said than done.

People may look at the work that the Lord is doing through you and give you credit for it, but you must, at all costs refuse to accept credit for these unsolicited accolades. The irony found in Christ's words are quite interesting in contrast to our way of thinking: "Woe unto you, when all men shall speak well of you: for so did their fathers to the false prophets," (Luke 6:26). No one wants to be associated with a false prophet, but Christ is merely reminding us that we are not here to please men, but God.

> For do I now persuade men, or God? or do I seek to please men? for if I yet pleased men, I should not be the servant of Christ. *Gal. 1:10*

THE POWER OF LIVING FOR OTHERS

In the following scripture, Paul eloquently describes the difference between law and grace: "For I know that in me (that is, in my flesh,) dwelleth no good thing: for to will is present with me; but how to perform that which is good I find not," (Rom. 7:18). Paul describes the inner struggles taking place between the desire to do what you know is right and an opposing force that wants to undermine that effort. This battle is being fought in the conscience of every human being. Lies and deceit serve as a barrier to recognizing and accepting the truth, even the truth about ourselves. It is imperative that you understand that in order to serve the Lord you should not look to mankind for rewards for your service. Serving the Lord involves serving mankind and being a servant to others.

The problem with Christians today is that we have a tendency to serve God intellectually and religiously. We've reduced Christianity to scripture memorization and catchy phrases which would make us a good candidate for Biblical Trivial Pursuit. But where is the holy passion? Where is that fire that burns within us to accomplish God's plan and purpose for our lives; the passion that keeps us on course, deafening us to the nagging secular distractions designed to prey on our weaknesses? The hope of heaven will escape us if we fail to exhibit the very essence of God's nature—His desire that we love one another.

CAN I GET A WITNESS? SHARING YOUR TESTIMONY

Having a short memory of your life before Christ is not conducive to healthy Christian growth. In order to effectively serve the Lord, we must remember how awful and empty we were apart from the knowledge of God. To acknowledge that we served our own selfish, unrestrained lusts and that those actions proved to be unfulfilling is liberating. Honesty in Christ frees us and releases the guilt that had stolen our self-esteem and eroded our self-pride. Our lusts not only carried us into places that we did not want to be, but made it impossible for us to deliver ourselves out of our predicament.

The Apostle Paul gives us an understanding of what it means to deny our contrary desires and how to supplant them with a divine nature of faith: "I am crucified with Christ: nevertheless I live; yet not I, but Christ liveth in me: and the life which I now live in the flesh I live by the faith of the Son of God, who loved me, and gave himself for me," (Gal. 2:20).

To serve the Lord is to restore the fallen virtues of integrity, honesty, righteousness, and holiness. In order to serve the Lord, we must adorn our lives with these virtues and lift them up as a banner in a crusade—unyielding and unrelenting. Society has grown weary of the constant reminders of its wayward state of consciousness. We must refuse to be silenced by the unpopularity of upholding Christian virtues, even among those from whom we seek acceptance and approval.

For we ourselves also were sometimes foolish, disobedient, deceived, serving divers lusts and pleasures, living in malice and envy, hateful, [and] hating one another. But after that the kindness and love of God our Saviour toward man appeared, Not by works of righteousness which we have done, but according to his mercy he saved us, by the washing of regeneration, and renewing of the Holy Ghost. *Titus 3:3–5*

Serving the Lord is not what I do, but rather who I am. You know that you are serving the Lord when you don't hesitate or stall for time when asked about your life choices as a Christian. You know you are serving the Lord when you look forward to sharing your views about your faith in Christ and genuinely offer God as a real solution to life's problems and fears.

Walking in the Light

Like anyone living in darkness, our initial response to light is to shield our eyes from the invading brightness. Once acclimated, the light that first stunned us reveals things we've hidden or even forgotten in our lives that now demand our immediate attention. How we implement the cleanup process in our lives will determine the effectiveness of our Christian walk.

The Bible describes light in the following way: "But all things that are reproved are made manifest by the light: for whatsoever doth make manifest is light," (Eph. 5:13). I love this biblical definition of light because it is so reflective of what it means to live a life of faith. If we are to serve the Lord, His light must shine through us and manifest the darkness of this world.

Setting the Example

To serve the Lord, you need to spiritually dress for success as this verse shows: "That he might present it to himself a glorious church, not having spot, or wrinkle, or any such thing; but that it should be holy and without blemish," (Eph. 5:27). Spots, by spiritual definition, are blatant transgressions against God. A wrinkle is something visible in your life that takes away from your witness for Christ. It needs to be ironed out as soon as possible. Blemishes are also visible transgressions and tarnish your appearance before God. A blemish on your Christian life may be a little subtler, yet still distracting.

Address those spots, wrinkles, and blemishes in your life so that you can truly represent the cleanliness that is expected from a child of God. Keep in mind that serving the Lord is not just putting away the filth of the flesh, but the answer of a pure conscience before God.

As believers, we must accept the daily challenges of Christian discipleship that uncover our strengths as well as our weaknesses. It is not enough to just refrain from the lurking darkness of temptations or to pretend to be obedient to God's commandments. Each day, we need to examine and purge our motives to make sure they are aligned with godly intentions.

Serving the Lord with sincerity and truth means that we must keep ourselves unspotted from the world. We must walk in the light of the word of God in such a way that no one can accuse us of wrongdoings that would cause His word to be blasphemed. This is what Paul was alluding to when he shared this with his son in the gospel, Titus: "To be discreet, chaste, keepers at home, good, obedient to their own husbands, that the word of God be not blasphemed," (Titus 2:5). Paul is saying that people have expectations of a follower of the faith and how they should carry themselves in and out of the home. When we profess that we are Christians and do not live accordingly, people will judge God because of our actions.

Surrendering Desires

When you are truly serving the Lord, you must not take consolation in the things that you don't do anymore, but rather the things that you don't desire to do anymore. The latter reflects the mystery of faith that is found in the surrendering and changing of our desires. This is when you know that you have crossed the demarcation point from having a religion to having a personal relationship with the Lord.

The Apostle Peter is saying that whatever force you surrender to, that force becomes your master: "...for of whom a man is overcome, of the same is he brought in bondage," (2 Pet. 2:19). This is the reason why some of you professed believers dance to the beat of a different drum. Who or what has overcome you? It's really very easy to determine; look at the enslaving habits that dominate your life and you will see your bondage.

> Be not overcome of evil, but overcome evil with good.
> *Rom. 12:21*

Sin does not reign in the lives of Christians once they have been overcome by Christ. The evil of this present time is a force to reckon with, but we are encouraged by the words of the well known Christian song; "Greater is he that is in me than he that is in the world." Sin does not reign in our mortal bodies because mortality has been swallowed up with immortality, even while we are still in these fleshly bodies. This is the beauty of holiness. When I surrender to the force of the Holy Spirit that is within me, there are things that I just cannot not do. Even though the struggle may still exist, my strengthened will enables me to claim the victory.

The Mystery of Faith

"For the flesh lusteth against the Spirit, and the Spirit against the flesh: and these are contrary the one to the other: so that ye cannot do the things that ye would," (Gal. 5:17). This passage describes the human struggle that plagues every believer yet consoles every born-again heart. This is the true mystery of faith that is still hidden from the eyes of those trapped in religious bondage.

> But if our gospel be hid, it is hid to them that are lost:

> In whom the god of this world hath blinded the minds
> of them which believe not, lest the light of the glori-
> ous gospel of Christ, who is the image of God, should
> shine unto them. *2 Cor. 4:3–4*

There is a war between God and Satan being fought for supreme rule over the souls of men. Because of the value of our souls, the price of defeat is too great. As Christians, we must recognize this bitter struggle, yet still mount up with the courage to prevail. Only courageous followers will know the true meaning of how to serve the Lord in spirit and truth.

Pastor Robinson's Sunday School Lesson

I Surrender All

Surrender literally means to give up something to another person. It means to relinquish something granted to you such as your power, possessions, and goals—even your life. This is what God commands and expects of us today. It is not enough for you to select what you want to surrender to God—God wants you to surrender all.

Phil. 3:7–8

7 But what things were gain to me, those I counted loss for Christ.

8 Yea doubtless, and I count all things but loss for the excellency of the knowledge of Christ Jesus my Lord: for whom I have suffered the loss of all things, and do count them but dung, that I may win Christ.

To surrender to the Lord is to surrender to His word. Whenever the light of God's word is revealed to you, you must submit in obedience without hesitation.

Jesus' full surrender to God is an example that we must follow. Jesus did not make a move without being instructed by God. As Christians, an honest assessment would probably reveal that we do not honestly seek God's guidance because we are not willing to surrender our will to his. How long do you think God will tolerate this type of so-called faith?

John 10:17–18

17 Therefore doth my Father love me, because I lay down my life, that I might take it again.

18 No man taketh it from me, but I lay it down of myself. I have power to lay it down, and I have power to take it again. This commandment have I received of my Father.

As a Christian, you too have the power of self-surrender. You choose to live a life of obedience and submission to God.

John 8:50

50 And I seek not mine own glory: there is one that seeketh and judgeth.

James 1:5–8

5 If any of you lack wisdom, let him ask of God, that giveth to all men liberally, and upbraideth not; and it shall be given him.

6 But let him ask in faith, nothing wavering: for he that wavereth is like a wave of the sea driven with the wind and tossed.

7 For let not that man think that he shall receive any thing of the Lord.

8 A double minded man is unstable in all his ways.

We can have as much Jesus in us as we choose to have. Stop making excuses. If you are weak in your faith it is because you choose to be weak by not fully surrendering to God. You have allowed Satan to deceive you into thinking that God is overlooking your slothfulness. The Lord can only use what is surrendered to him and it is either all or nothing.

Gen. 19:26

26 But his wife looked back from behind him, and she became a pillar of salt.

Luke 9:62

62 Jesus said unto him, No man, having put his hand to the plough, and looking back, is fit for the kingdom of God.

In the following verses we see the dangers of not surrendering to God.

Acts 8:18–24

18 And when Simon saw that through laying on of the apostles' hands the Holy Ghost was given, he offered them money,

19 Saying, Give me also this power, that on whomsoever I lay hands, he may receive the Holy Ghost.

20 But Peter said unto him, Thy money perish with thee, because thou hast thought that the gift of God may be purchased with money.

21 Thou hast neither part nor lot in this matter: for thy heart is not right in the sight of God.

22 Repent therefore of this thy wickedness, and pray God, if perhaps the thought of thine heart may be forgiven thee.

23 For I perceive that thou art in the gall of bitterness, and in the bond of iniquity.

24 Then answered Simon, and said, Pray ye to the Lord for me, that none of these things which ye have spoken come upon me.

John 12:2–6

2 There they made him a supper; and Martha served: but Lazarus was one of them that sat at the table with him.

3 Then took Mary a pound of ointment of spikenard, very costly, and anointed the feet of Jesus, and wiped his feet with her hair: and the house was filled with the odour of the ointment.

4 Then saith one of his disciples, Judas Iscariot, Simon's son, which should betray him,

5 Why was not this ointment sold for three hundred pence, and given to the poor?

6 This he said, not that he cared for the poor; but because he was a thief, and had the bag, and bare what was put therein.

As Christians, we will never reach spiritual maturity until we agree to a total surrender to God. The following verses exemplify this.

Luke 14:28–33

28 For which of you, intending to build a tower, sitteth not down first, and counteth the cost, whether he have sufficient to finish it?

29 Lest haply, after he hath laid the foundation, and is not able to finish it, all that behold it begin to mock him,

30 Saying, This man began to build, and was not able to finish.

31 Or what king, going to make war against another king, sitteth not down first, and consulteth whether he be able with ten thousand to meet him that cometh against him with twenty thousand?

32 Or else, while the other is yet a great way off, he sendeth an ambassage, and desireth conditions of peace.

33 So likewise, whosoever he be of you that forsaketh not all that he hath, he cannot be my disciple.

1 Cor 6:19–20

19 What? know ye not that your body is the temple of the Holy Ghost which is in you, which ye have of God, and ye are not your own?

20 For ye are bought with a price: therefore glorify God in your body, and in your spirit, which are God's.

Rom. 6:12–17

12 Let not sin therefore reign in your mortal body, that ye should obey it in the lusts thereof.

13 Neither yield ye your members as instruments of unrighteousness unto sin: but yield yourselves unto God, as those that are alive from the dead, and your members as instruments of righteousness unto God.

14 For sin shall not have dominion over you: for ye are not under the law, but under grace.

15 What then? shall we sin, because we are not under the law, but under grace? God forbid.

16 Know ye not, that to whom ye yield yourselves servants to obey, his servants ye are to whom ye obey; whether of sin unto death, or of obedience unto righteousness?

17 But God be thanked, that ye were the servants of sin, but ye have obeyed from the heart that form of doctrine which was delivered you.

Consider what it means to be crucified with Christ:

Gal. 2:20

20 I am crucified with Christ: nevertheless I live; yet not I, but Christ liveth in me: and the life which I now live in the flesh I live by the faith of the Son of God, who loved me, and gave himself for me.

A stronghold is an area of your life that you refuse to surrender to Christ. This may be an inward or an outward sin that you enjoy and still struggle with. You must release that sin and surrender your body, soul, and spirit to Christ.

2 Cor. 10:4–5

4 (For the weapons of our warfare are not carnal, but mighty through God to the pulling down of strong holds;)

5 Casting down imaginations, and every high thing that exalteth itself against the knowledge of God, and bringing into captivity every thought to the obedience of Christ.

USING MY MUSICAL TALENT FOR JESUS CHRIST

BRO. WALTER D. PETITT

I want to first give praise to my Lord and Savoir, Jesus Christ, for his mercy, salvation, and grace. As a youth, I remember being around music, bands, and musicians all the time. My father's side of the family is musically inclined. My only uncle on my mother's side is a drummer as well. With no formal training, I started playing drums at the age of 7. By the age of 8, I was playing drums with talented adult musicians.

In 1988, after moving back to Abilene, Texas from Austin, Texas, I joined a gospel quartet group called The Voices of Heaven. I played drums for seven years with them before we lost our bassist. I transitioned to bass guitar and piano. While playing the bass and piano, I noticed I wasn't as talented as my father and uncles, which made me very uneasy.

Our gospel group traveled all over Texas. Sometimes we got paid, but it was barely enough to cover gas. The members of the churches and venues where we played often provided food and shelter. At that time, you couldn't make as much money playing gospel music as you could playing hip hop music, rap, and R&B music, so we pretty much played for free.

In 1995, I was blessed with some studio equipment. I started producing and recording in an old building in Abilene, Texas. I recorded our gospel group and other artists. In 1999, I was blessed with newer studio equipment, so I opened a bigger studio. I formed a record label, signed a rap group, and developed other artists. Some of the artists I developed were career criminals and drug dealers. At that time, I chose the studio and my new career as a producer over my family. This decision caused a division in my marriage and I was estranged from my family for a few months.

I began living at the studio and bathing from a bucket. I was a sinner, but I promised God that I would put Him first, get back into church, and put no one on earth above my wife and daughters. I asked God to restore my family and He did. My wife and I were blessed with a son in May, 2000. Jesus Christ also blessed me with a job in Austin that same year. We didn't know it then, but He was setting us up to meet a God-fearing pastor and to become part of a church family.

My immediate family lives in Austin, and after being around my father, my uncles, and top 40 bands, I was tempted to get back into worldly music. I remembered the promise I made to God. I knew that the Lord could take my family away again, so I didn't want to take a chance.

Sometimes, I played drums for my uncle Jack's church when their drummer couldn't attend services. We were invited to play at a small church on the south side of Austin for the pastor's anniversary. Playing that night at that church was a life-changing experience for me. I went home and told my wife that I had finally found a church for us. The next Sunday, my family and I visited the church, which is now our church home. Under the guidance of Pastor Salem Robinson, Jr. and the word of God, and after listening to the testimonies of our Brothers and Sisters in Christ, the Lord saved our souls, our marriage, and our kids from hell.

I planned to join the choir as a singer, but that changed when the choir directors found out I could play bass guitar and drums. I really didn't want to play bass guitar for the church, because I hadn't played bass for a long time and gospel music is hard to play. I wanted to quit playing those instruments and just sing. But God had other plans for me, and those plans had me playing the bass guitar! I am the bassist for the church and I play the drums when needed.

My old desires to use my talents to play worldly music have changed. I've found out that serving God and using my talents to give glory back to God is worth more than gold. Musicians at other churches get paid hundreds of dollars to play each Sunday. I'm often asked if I get paid to play for our church. My answer is no. Jesus Christ has blessed me with things I couldn't acquire as a sinner and I owe Him everything. If I never receive another blessing from this day forward I can truly say that I've been blessed. I will continue to use my talents to glorify God through His son, my Lord and Savior, Jesus Christ.

Using My Gifts and Talents for the Lord

Bro. Salem "Trey" Robinson III

I can remember as a young child having a love for music that continued to grow with me into adulthood. I remember my family's piano that I would often play. I taught myself chords and fingering and I would make and arrange songs. I played by ear and I could easily hear if the notes weren't right. After I got comfortable performing in front of my family, I would entertain our guests and put on mini concerts. When I got into junior high school, it was natural that I would enroll in piano and choir courses, which further developed my knowledge and abilities.

Entering my late teenage years, I got involved with gospel youth groups within the church. I often had lead roles that included rapping, acting, and singing. I loved the energy that we displayed when performing, but at the time, I didn't understand the difference between performing for man and praising the Lord.

As I've grown in my Christian walk I've learned that when I performed, the satisfaction was all for myself as if my talents are something that I'd achieved alone. When my efforts and talents are used to praise the Lord, all the glory and honor goes to Him. I fully understand now that it is because of Him that I have this talent.

When I was in my early twenties, a friend that I grew up with in the church approached me with the idea of starting an R&B group. At this time I was a Christian and understood my obligation to God. My father, who is a minister, would always say "the music today is not decent like it used to be." I have to agree with my father. Women are often disrespected and sexually exploited in today's music.

While I agreed to sing with the group, I had a few conditions. We both agreed we wouldn't disrespect women or have any cursing in our songs. Later, we signed with a label that provided us with a manager who booked us on numerous shows. We performed in clubs, at festivals, at weddings and parties, and other events.

At the time, I didn't see anything wrong with the music we sang since we both understood our limits. Now that I look back at some of the venues where we performed, I can see that what I was doing was unacceptable Christian behavior. Although I never took part in the drinking or smoking that went on at the events where we performed, I've learned that as a Christian, I wasn't setting a good example by being in that environment. My gifts and talents weren't being used for the glory of God in the clubs; it was really being used for the devil.

I will always fondly remember the years I spent being part of the singing group and the pact we made to show integrity and decency. I'm thankful that my childhood friend was open to this arrangement and he'll always be a dear friend. However, as life's changes came about and I became aware of the Lord's will for my life, our group eventually dissolved. I know that God works everything out in His time. We both ventured towards solo projects and I started producing both gospel music and love songs.

My experiences have taught me that there are ways to be decent in a song even when it is not a gospel song. I often compose songs that are clearly about relationships and love and I strongly feel that love songs and gospel songs are sometimes closely aligned. The difference now is that I don't play in clubs or in an environment that would make my Christian light grow dim. With no formal training on any instrument, I've still managed to produce two gospel albums and love songs with the help of the Lord.

Being taught as a Christian at Dunn's Memorial has helped me learn and understand how to use my gifts and talents for the Lord.

I've taken formal vocal training but I know I wouldn't be able to sing one note without God having given me these gifts. I believe by using my talents for the Lord, He has given me even more gifts to be used for His glory. In addition to playing the keyboard and composing beats, I now play drums and guitar for the church choir. As I grow in faith, I pray that my gifts and talents will always be used to God's glory and honor, because I know that only what I do for Christ will last.

Chapter Four: Overcoming Fear
ANGELA'S TESTIMONY

If you are frozen in place, unable to move forward in your life or burdened with worry, fear is the underlying cause of your troubles. Fear and faith don't mix. Fear is the opposite of faith, and you can't love or serve the Lord, yourself, or others if you are fearful. Worry is the result of fear and concrete evidence of a lack of faith in God. As long as Satan can convince you that you're all alone with your burdens and your problems, fear and worry will always be present in your life. I'm talking about carnal fear, the kind that dwells in the heart of a person who refuses to put their trust in God.

While fear caused by Satan is the enemy of all Christians, there is another type of fear that can aid Christians in their journey—the fear of God. The biblical definition of godly fear is found in Psalms: "The fear of the Lord is the beginning of wisdom: a good understanding have all they that do his commandments: his praise endureth for ever," (Ps. 111:10).

I've learned that spiritual fear is a love for God, a respect for His power, and obedience to His commandments. I first had to overcome my carnal fears to be able to understand and obtain a spiritual fear of the Lord.

Spiritual fear will empower you to be obedient to His commandments—no matter what the cost. It will transform you into a bold warrior for Christ. The more obedient you are to the Lord, the more faith He gives you to overcome your carnal fears. He'll bless you with an unwavering faith and the grace to do His will, no matter what the challenge may be.

Even though I was calling myself a Christian, carnal fear had paralyzed me. I worried about everything from how we were going to pay our bills to my health, our future, and on and on. I was so burdened with fear and worry that I couldn't rest or focus on anything except myself and my problems. Of course, I put on a smile and went about my day as if nothing was wrong. It was exhausting to pretend that I was trusting in the Lord, when in reality, I wasn't.

I prayed constantly about all of my problems. I kept reminding the Lord of what I needed, when I needed it, and how much I needed it—as if He didn't know! My prayers at that time were all about me and my carnal needs. Fear will erase anything positive from your mind and flood your spirit with negative thoughts. Fear will narrow your focus so that all you can think about is yourself. I forgot about all the many, many blessings that the Lord had rained down upon my life. I forgot that He had brought me through each and every trial. I forgot that He was my friend and that He loved and cared for me.

I've had many life-changing moments while attending Sunday School and Bible study or while listening to sermons on a Sunday morning. One Sunday, the choir was singing "My God Can Do Anything!" I clapped and sang along, but if you looked at my spiritual life, it was obvious that I didn't believe a word I was singing! If I truly believed that "my God can do anything," why was I filled with so much stress and anxiety? Why couldn't I sleep at night? Fear had a death grip on my mind and my spirit. My faith that "God can do anything" was slowly slipping away.

Then, as He has done so many times over the years, God used Pastor Robinson to give me a spiritual wakeup call. Pastor Robinson's sermon that Sunday helped me to overcome my fears. His sermon was titled "Is Worry A Sin?"

Have you ever been listening to the word of God and wondered if the pastor was directing his comments to you? That's how I felt on that particular Sunday! Pastor Robinson explained that the Old English definition of worry is "to strangle." That was the perfect definition of how I felt at that time. Fear had a stranglehold on me. My faith was gasping for air and slowly dying. I was wrapped up in worry, and my mind was clouded with all of the burdens I was unnecessarily bearing. I couldn't breathe.

I had to learn what the gospel song "Take Your Burdens to the Lord and Leave Them There," really meant. He said leave them there! I kept going back to the cross to get my burdens because the Lord wasn't moving fast enough to suit me! I kept praying the same prayer over and over again because I didn't have enough faith to believe that the Lord hears our prayers and is more than able to sustain us in our time of need.

I used to have a long list of carnal needs that I asked the Lord to fulfill. I was so self-centered that I didn't have too much time to pray for anyone else! My fears ruled my prayer life, preventing me from using that time to have a heartfelt conversation with the Lord, to be grateful, or to address the spiritual things I needed help to understand or to overcome. My fears and worries made me forget that I didn't have to carry my burdens alone. The Lord was waiting patiently for me to be obedient, overcome my fears, and turn my cares over to Him.

I'll never forget one night when I was praying, yet again, for money for this or that, or for the Lord to make a way for us. I heard a voice in my spirit say "I have already taken care of that! Just be thankful!" I started to laugh. I had been so fearful that we were going to lose all of our possessions, that I had forgotten the lesson I had learned so vividly at the age of 10. The Lord is mindful of His children, even when they are in the pitiful, fearful condition that I was in, because He knows our hearts. If He can take care of sparrows, surely He can take care of us. I stopped praying, got into the bed, and went to sleep. To this day, when the devil tries to flood my mind with fear, I think back to that night and say to myself, "He takes care of sparrows!" God is more than able, in His own time, to lift our burdens and deliver us from every trial and tribulation.

I've learned how to pray and just be thankful! Instead of asking the Lord for worldly comforts, now when I pray, I thank Him for what he has done and by faith, for what He will do as He sees fit in my life.

Just when I felt like I had overcome my carnal fears by the grace of God, the Lord revealed to me that I still had a fear of man. I do a tremendous amount of public speaking for workshops, conferences, and television. I've come to realize that part of my service to the Lord is taking every opportunity He provides me with to share the good news of the gospel of Jesus Christ with others.

I had been doing public appearances as an author or as a chef for almost 20 years and never really mentioned anything about the fact that I'm a Christian. I've had the opportunity to speak before large crowds, many of which were probably seeking the Lord or needed a boost in their faith. Because I was afraid of what people might say about me if I talked about being a Christian, I never told my audiences anything about my beliefs. When asked how I managed to have such a successful career as an author or how I got into doing a television cooking show, I never gave glory to the Lord or explained that He is the one who has blessed me with the gifts and talents I possess.

The key to overcoming fear is to replace it with faith. The way to increase your faith is to be obedient to the will and the word of God. When I finally realized that God was and always will be in control, that my purpose in life is to do His will, and that if I'm obedient, He will always make a way for me, my fear of man evaporated.

Now, whether I am speaking before a crowd, doing a cooking demonstration on national television, or signing my books at a bookstore, I pray and ask the Lord to give me the words to say so that I can glorify Him. He always provides me with the inspiration and faith to inspire my audiences. After I've shared my faith with my audience, I often receive compliments about my courage to take a stand for the Lord.

From time to time, an audience member will approach me quietly, wanting to ask questions or talk about their own walk with the Lord. I've noticed that sometimes they whisper, as if it's a secret, when they tell me that they're Christian, too. I refuse to whisper about my faith. If you're truly living a Christian life according to the word of God, and you know what He has done for you, testify to His goodness! You need to be bold for the Lord, without any fear, and take a stand for what you believe.

I've learned how to conquer carnal fear through faith in the Lord and the blessing of prayer. I've learned that faith is like a muscle; when you put it to use against something that seems too heavy to lift, it grows stronger. I've left the old, fearful Angela behind and I've become a warrior for Christ. Now, I have a spiritual fear of the Lord, and He has increased my faith.

I've entered into a different phase of my Christian life and I love it. I enjoy sharing my testimony about how the Lord has worked in my life. I've learned how to overcome my fear of man through the power of faith and developed a spiritual fear of the Lord. I still have challenges and trials in my life, but now I face each situation with faith, not fear.

As strange as it may sound, I've come to rejoice when I'm faced with a trial because I know that the Lord is going to bring me through in a miraculous way. I know that I will never be able to fully express my gratitude to the Lord for all the many blessings He has bestowed upon me—but that doesn't stop me from trying! Now and throughout all of eternity, I'll testify of His goodness anywhere He wants me to—boldly, and without any fear.

Comments by Pastor Salem Robinson, Jr.

It is human nature to fear the things we don't understand. Our minds have an incredible ability to fill in the blanks concerning life. Unfortunately, we fill in the blanks with a dismal, pessimistic picture that causes us to fear. The fear of the unknown will spawn hypothetical scenarios that paralyze us from attempting those things that have not been safely choreographed. This is a recipe for not only a boring life, but an unhappy one as well. There is truth in the old saying, "anything worth having is worth fighting for." The fear of failure will either motivate you to succeed or prep you for failure.

Gaining victory over your fear does not mean you are no longer frightened, it only means you are no longer controlled by it. You will never prosper as a child of God until you stop being afraid to perform what is expected of you before God. Your spiritual prosperity is tied to your faith and courage in Christ.

Overcoming the Fear of Man Through the Power of Faith

Are you a fearful person? What holy zeal do you demonstrate? Are you willing to act like a Christian, risking the disapproval of others? If you cannot identify your passion, not even for God, you have not overcome fear. You're probably "just trying to survive"— the motto of those living in fear.

I have heard it said that if you truly fear God, you fear nothing else. To discover the truth in this statement, we need to re-examine our faith in God and reconsider all of the objects of our fears. The Bible sheds light on the role of fear in our lives: "Then the same day at evening, being the first day of the week, when the doors were shut where the disciples were assembled for fear of the Jews, came Jesus and stood in the midst, and saith unto them, Peace be unto you," (John 20:19).

During Christ's arrest, trial, and crucifixion His disciples were overwhelmed by fear. They hid together behind locked doors and pondered what their fate might be in the days ahead. As Christians, this type of behavior must not be repeated. Have you ever locked the doors to your heart because of fear and somehow miraculously Jesus just walked in anyway? He has been known to make such unannounced appearances, but don't expect for Him to continue this type of visitation if you are too afraid to invite Him in yourself.

The Bible also tells us that "The fear of man bringeth a snare; but whoso puteth his trust in the Lord shall be safe," (Prov. 29:25). Both of these sayings regarding fear are true on their own, but they are even more powerful when linked together. "The fear of man bringeth a snare," is a truth which experience has taught many of us. Trying to please men will cause you to fail before God. "Whoso puteth his trust in the Lord shall be safe," has also been found to be true by those who have tested it. Putting these two thoughts into one proverb provides a deep insight about overcoming fear—the fear of man causes you to make bad life choices but if you trust in God, you are guaranteed to avoid those snares.

The fear of losing human acceptance is what we call the fear of man. There are so many people who have no fear of God but have a great fear of man. They break the laws of God without any fear of the consequences yet they are afraid to break the laws of man because they dread the punishment. They are not afraid of hell, yet they are afraid of what men may say or do. How men can fear public opinion more than an eternity in hell is still a mystery to me.

> And fear not them which kill the body, but are not able to kill the soul: but rather fear him which is able to destroy both soul and body in hell. *Matt 10:28*

In the following passage, Jesus heals despite a family's fear:

> And they asked them, saying, Is this your son, who ye say was born blind? how then doth he now see? His parents answered them and said, we know that this is

our son, and that he was born blind: But by what means he now seeth, we know not; or who hath opened his eyes, we know not: he is of age; ask him: he shall speak for himself. These words spake his parents, because they feared the Jews: for the Jews had agreed already, that if any man did confess that he was Christ, he should be put out of the synagogue. Therefore said his parents, He is of age; ask him. *John 9:19–23*

Look at the fear of these parents—their son was born blind and Jesus healed him, but since Jesus wasn't well received among the hypocritical Jewish community of the day, they chose to refrain from giving glory to God. Why couldn't these parents just give glory to God for the miracle He performed on their child? It's because they were fearful that the community would be angry with them! They denied the wonderful work of God and put the responsibility back on their son. This type of fear is still prevalent in families today. Parents push the responsibility onto their children for everything because they are too fearful to take a stand.

TRUSTING GOD BEYOND OUR FEARS

For God hath not given us the spirit of fear; but of power, and of love, and of a sound mind. *2 Tim. 1:7*

Faith and fear are opposites, yet they are often both found dwelling within us. Where one is dominant the other is dormant. Just the way we use our faith to distance us from the stresses of this life, fear and anxieties can also be dispelled by your faith in God. Don't be guilty of doing nothing but expecting everything—fear will stop you from using what was entrusted to you.

As Americans, we enjoy a religious freedom that is unparalleled in the world. We have gifted ministers, teachers, and evangelists that can expound the word of God with grace. We are the most preached to and preached at nation on earth, yet we fulfill the words of the Apostle Paul, "They have a form of godliness but deny the power thereof," (2 Tim. 3:5).

The absence of conviction has left a gaping hole that Satan has filled with doubt and fear. People are not counting up the cost to be Christians anymore. They are simply joining religious institutions that never challenge their conscience to believe in righteousness and true holiness. The power of faith is missing! Therefore, faith without trust defaults back to the frailty of human fear that finds a comfortable seat within the pews of spiritually defeated churches.

LOVE CONQUERS FEAR

> There is no fear in love; but perfect love casteth out fear: because fear hath torment. He that feareth is not made perfect in love. *1 John 4:18*

When we love God with all of our heart, soul, mind, and strength, and love our neighbors as ourselves, we receive the power to inoculate ourselves against the infection of fear. We become so busy trying to love and please God that we actually become immune to the hindrance of our previous fears. When God's power isn't present in our lives, we are tormented by our inability to deal effectively with our fears. We rehearse over and over again the reasons why it seems as though failure is inevitable despite our desire to be obedient to God.

You must learn to deal with fear like you would any other bully—you stand up, face it, and refuse to run or to make excuses. Without trust in God, you will always look small in your own eyes before your adversary. As Christians, if we are to overcome our fears, we must see the enemy through the eyes of Caleb:

> And Caleb stilled the people before Moses, and said, Let us go up at once, and possess it; for we are well able to overcome it. But the men that went up with

him said, We be not able to go up against the people; for they are stronger than we. And they brought up an evil report of the land which they had searched unto the children of Israel, saying, The land, through which we have gone to search it, is a land that eateth up the inhabitants thereof; and all the people that we saw in it are men of a great stature. And there we saw the giants, the sons of Anak, which come of the giants: and we were in our own sight as grasshoppers, and so we were in their sight. *Num. 13:30–33*

Real faith in God shrinks our enemies to a size that can be easily handled. Remember, after Jesus Christ was raised from the dead but before His ascension back into heaven, He said "All power is given unto me in heaven and in earth," (Matt. 28:18). Jesus Christ died so that we can claim the victory over every one of our pesky fears. If we are to truly overcome our fears, we must learn to trust God beyond our fears. We must always surrender to the conviction of conscience because there is no such thing as a cowardly Christian.

Pastor Robinson's Sunday School Lesson
The Crippling Emotion of Fear

Phobias are irrational fears that compel us to do irresponsible things or inhibit us from doing what we should. As Christians, phobias can indicate a lack of faith in God. The number one reason Christians don't share their faith is the fear of man or, more specifically, the fear of rejection and failure.

We pray concerning our problems, but many times our prayers are motivated by fear, not faith. "Lord, if you don't heal me, I'll die," "If you don't give me a job, I'll lose all of my possessions," etc. God doesn't want us to be sick, hungry, or unable to pay our bills, but as long as fear is the motive for our prayers, I don't believe He will answer. God responds to faith, not fear.

Death is the greatest mystery of all. Since there are plenty of distractions out there, ignoring death can be easy. Often, the only time people think about death is when they become seriously ill, when someone close to them dies, or when there is a major calamity. Fear will prevent you from experiencing God's plan for your life. Jesus faced death with courage. He welcomed it, knowing that His death would not lead to His destruction, but to victory. In all that Christ did, He was fearless. Let us meditate on the following verses that show us the destructive power of fear and the redemptive power of trusting God.

Heb. 13:5–6

5 Let your conversation be without covetousness; and be content with such things as ye have: for he hath said, I will never leave thee, nor forsake thee.

6 So that we may boldly say, The Lord is my helper, and I will not fear what man shall do unto me.

2 Tim. 1:6–7

6 Wherefore I put thee in remembrance that thou stir up the gift of God, which is in thee by the putting on of my hands.

7 For God hath not given us the spirit of fear; but of power, and of love, and of a sound mind.

Matt. 25:24–30

24 Then he which had received the one talent came and said, Lord, I knew thee that thou art an hard man, reaping where thou hast not sown, and gathering where thou hast not strawed:

25 And I was afraid, and went and hid thy talent in the earth: lo, there thou hast that is thine.

26 His lord answered and said unto him, Thou wicked and slothful servant, thou knewest that I reap where I sowed not, and gather where I have not strawed:

27 Thou oughtest therefore to have put my money to the exchangers, and then at my coming I should have received mine own with usury.

28 Take therefore the talent from him, and give it unto him which hath ten talents.

29 For unto every one that hath shall be given, and he shall have abundance: but from him that hath not shall be taken away even that which he hath.

30 And cast ye the unprofitable servant into outer darkness: there shall be weeping and gnashing of teeth.

Luke 14:28–30

28 For which of you, intending to build a tower, sitteth not down first, and counteth the cost, whether he have sufficient to finish it?

29 Lest haply, after he hath laid the foundation, and is not able to finish it, all that behold it begin to mock him,

30 Saying, This man began to build, and was not able to finish.

Mary Magdalene told the disciples that she had seen the Lord, but during Christ's arrest, trial, and crucifixion, His disciples were overwhelmed by fear. They hid together behind locked doors and pondered what their fate might be in the days ahead. They were afraid of the people, particularly the religious leaders who put Jesus to death. They were dealing with the perceived failure and re-assessing their faith. They were even afraid for their very lives! After all, if their master had been falsely accused, tried, and executed, certainly they could be next.

John 20:17–23

17 Jesus saith unto her, Touch me not; for I am not yet ascended to my Father: but go to my brethren, and say unto them, I ascend unto my Father, and your Father; and to my God, and your God.

18 Mary Magdalene came and told the disciples that she had seen the Lord, and that he had spoken these things unto her.

19 Then the same day at evening, being the first day of the week, when the doors were shut where the disciples were assembled for fear of the Jews, came Jesus and stood in the midst, and saith unto them, Peace be unto you.

20 And when he had so said, he shewed unto them his hands and his side. Then were the disciples glad, when they saw the Lord.

21 Then said Jesus to them again, Peace be unto you: as my Father hath sent me, even so send I you.

22 And when he had said this, he breathed on them, and saith unto them, Receive ye the Holy Ghost:

23 Whose soever sins ye remit, they are remitted unto them; and whose soever sins ye retain, they are retained.

Faith allows you to move into uncharted territory with full confidence that God is already there waiting for you.

Acts 4:1–20

1 And as they spake unto the people, the priests, and the captain of the temple, and the Sadducees, came upon them,

2 Being grieved that they taught the people, and preached through Jesus the resurrection from the dead.

3 And they laid hands on them, and put them in hold unto the next day: for it was now eventide.

4 Howbeit many of them which heard the word believed; and the number of the men was about five thousand.

5 And it came to pass on the morrow, that their rulers, and elders, and scribes,

6 And Annas the high priest, and Caiaphas, and John, and Alexander, and as many as were of the kindred of the high priest, were gathered together at Jerusalem.

7 And when they had set them in the midst, they asked, By what power, or by what name, have ye done this?

8 Then Peter, filled with the Holy Ghost, said unto them, Ye rulers of the people, and elders of Israel,

9 If we this day be examined of the good deed done to the impotent man, by what means he is made whole;

10 Be it known unto you all, and to all the people of Israel, that by the name of Jesus Christ of Nazareth, whom ye crucified, whom God raised from the dead, even by him doth this man stand here before you whole.

11 This is the stone which was set at nought of you builders, which is become the head of the corner.

12 Neither is there salvation in any other: for there is none other name under heaven given among men, whereby we must be saved.

13 Now when they saw the boldness of Peter and John, and perceived that they were unlearned and ignorant men, they marvelled; and they took knowledge of them, that they had been with Jesus.

14 And beholding the man which was healed standing with them, they could say nothing against it.

15 But when they had commanded them to go aside out of the council, they conferred among themselves,

16 Saying, What shall we do to these men? for that indeed a notable miracle hath been done by them is manifest to all them that dwell in Jerusalem; and we cannot deny it.

17 But that it spread no further among the people, let us straitly threaten them, that they speak henceforth to no man in this name.

18 And they called them, and commanded them not to speak at all nor teach in the name of Jesus.

19 But Peter and John answered and said unto them, Whether it be right in the sight of God to hearken unto you more than unto God, judge ye.

20 For we cannot but speak the things which we have seen and heard.

In a little over a month, the disciples were transformed from the inside out. Peter and John were arrested for boldly proclaiming the resurrection of Christ from the street corners. Although the very people they had been hiding from commanded them to stop preaching, they refused.

What gave these men the boldness to preach about the risen Christ publicly? Is it possible that Peter had a flashback of the time that he walked on water? They took their eyes off of themselves and their circumstances and placed them on the risen Christ. They let go of their fear of man and put their trust in God.

Overcoming the Fear of Witnessing

Just as the disciples overcame their fears, we, as Christians, must also overcome our fear of witnessing. The following verses attest to the importance of witnessing.

John 7:10–13

10 But when his brethren were gone up, then went he also up unto the feast, not openly, but as it were in secret.

11 Then the Jews sought him at the feast, and said, Where is he?

12 And there was much murmuring among the people concerning him: for some said, He is a good man: others said, Nay; but he deceiveth the people.

13 Howbeit no man spake openly of him for fear of the Jews.

During a survey given at a Billy Graham training session, participants were asked, "What is your greatest hindrance to witnessing?" Nine percent said they were too busy to remember to do it. Twenty-eight percent felt the lack of real information to share. Twelve percent said their own lives prevented them from speaking as they should. The largest group was the 51% whose biggest problem was the fear of how other people would react! The greatest fears of becoming a strong witness for Jesus Christ are fear of rejection, fear of embarrassment, and the fear of being labelled as a fanatic.

John 11:43–44

43 And when he thus had spoken, he cried with a loud voice, Lazarus, come forth.

44 And he that was dead came forth, bound hand and foot with gravecloths: and his face was bound about with a napkin. Jesus saith unto them, Loose him, and let him go.

Lazarus was now a living man but still clothed in the garments of death. There are many professing Christians who have been made alive by the grace of Jesus Christ but continue to wear their grave clothes out of fear.

John 12:9–11

9 Much people of the Jews therefore knew that he was there: and they came not for Jesus' sake only, but that they might see Lazarus also, whom he had raised from the dead.

10 But the chief priests consulted that they might put Lazarus also to death;

11 Because that by reason of him, many of the Jews went away, and believed on Jesus.

Rom. 13:13–14

13 Let us walk honestly, as in the day; not in rioting and drunkenness, not in chambering and wantonness, not in strife and envying.

14 But put ye on the Lord Jesus Christ, and make not provision for the flesh, to fulfill the lusts thereof.

What happens if you try to put on Christ over your gravecloths?

Mark 5:15–19

15 And they come to Jesus, and see him that was possessed with the devil, and had the legion, sitting, and clothed, and in his right mind: and they were afraid.

16 And they that saw it told them how it befell to him that was possessed with the devil, and also concerning the swine.

17 And they began to pray him to depart out of their coasts.

18 And when he was come into the ship, he that had been possessed with the devil prayed him that he might be with him.

19 Howbeit Jesus suffered him not, but saith unto him, Go home to thy friends, and tell them how great things the Lord hath done for thee, and hath had compassion on thee.

I Say Bring it On

Sis. Essi Eargle

For 22 years I was a servant of Satan. I was in bondage; an incontinent creature, full of filth for as long as I can remember. In sin, I ran from every problem and every true reflection of what I had become through drugs, alcohol, and perversion. And this person inside of me who had a little desire to try and be somebody began to slip away. I had no morals, I had no self-esteem, I had no money, no job, no place of my own, and no understanding of the phrase "no, I'm not going to do that." It makes me ill to look back at my sinful life and some of the things I involved myself in.

On August 13th, 1999, I accepted Christ through the preached word of Jesus Christ by an elect minister named Salem Robinson, Jr. When I surrendered all by the grace of God I received the Holy Spirit, through faith in the death, burial, and resurrection of Jesus Christ. My whole life changed. I now strive for perfection according to God. The Lord has blessed me to have the best sleep I've ever had in my life. I feel special as a chosen elect of God and Christ. Under the guidance of true Christians, I began to grow.

To be a Christian is to be honored—this is the best life and life after death anyone could ever have. And I marvel at the devil, when he's in people, and sometimes I have to even laugh. By God through Christ I have been empowered to be able to say no to my former master, who was taking me to hell, not for riches, but in poverty. I was going to hell, but the Lord reached down and saved me. The devil gets in people, and thinks that he can shake me but I say greater is he that is in me. BRING IT ON.

The devil gets people who are in darkness to try and bring opposition to the light that shines on sin through me, but I say it is an honor to be a Christian. BRING IT ON.

Uh oh, what is this? The devil is in members of my biological family who expect me to give them so called respect by condoning and participating in sin. But I say the blood of Christ who delivered me from sin can deliver you, I'm not going to take my salvation lightly to please you. I say there be no blood thicker than the blood of Christ. BRING IT ON.

Lord Jesus give me the grace to be honest with myself in deciphering between persecution and the consequences of an unwise decision. With an unwise decision, Lord I repent, please grow me in grace and wisdom. But when I know for sure persecution awaits me because of my religion, I say, BRING IT ON.

The Lord is with me when I submit to God through Christ, I am protected. I say, BRING IT ON.

I am convinced there is nothing the devil can do to make me return to my old sinful life, separating me from Christ. I say, BRING IT ON.

Through Christ I am more than a conqueror, I say, BRING IT ON.

I fear God and if he be for me, who can be against me. I say, BRING IT ON.

The devil in people can do whatever he wishes, but by the grace of God, he will never have my joy and he will never have my soul. I fear not the one that can kill this body, but God and Jesus Christ who saved my soul.

Through Christ I am a soldier. I say, BRING IT ON.

Overcoming Fear

Sis. Terri C. Hargrove

 On August 26, 2005, I left my home in New Orleans
for a weekend stay,
Not knowing Hurricane Katrina was on its way.
During my visit in Covington, there was prediction of a storm,
But there, the weather seemed like the norm.
On August 29th, Katrina hit and there were a series of events;
I lost my car, my home, and most of its contents.
Though I wasn't in New Orleans, I heard many horrible stories.
But I soon realized that I had very few worries.
My life had been spared from the storm's fierce magnitude,
I give God the glory and much gratitude.
Some former residents of New Orleans had to confront new
fears and dangers,
Nevertheless, my family has made friends out of total strangers.
I will not say that I was misplaced,
Wherever I live, I'll still be in the Christian race.
We moved and became connected with our neighbor's church.
Yes, Dunn's Memorial in Austin, Texas ended my search.
At this church, the word of God is being taught,
And my church family provides us with the love that we sought.
Hurricane Katrina caused great devastation,
But in Christ, there is still reason for celebration.
It's Jesus who strengthens and takes care of me,
Therefore, I have the peace of God for others to see.
Overcoming fear is one of God's many blessings,
It makes us keep trusting, praying, and progressing.
To God be the glory!

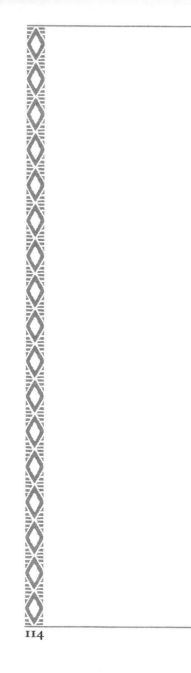

Chapter Five: Healing
ANGELA'S TESTIMONY

You may be wondering why there is so much sickness in the world, or why God allows illness, especially when it comes to His people. I've been blessed to be fairly healthy throughout my life, but each and every one of my ailments, illnesses, and hospitalizations have been part of the plan of God. I've learned that when illness befalls a Christian, it is the love and the divine will of God.

Throughout my Christian life, I've often needed a reality check. I get them from God in many forms, including sickness. Sometimes, you can hear the Lord better when you can't move out of bed! There have been numerous times that the Lord was trying to direct me or using others to speak to me, and I just wouldn't listen. I was too busy being self-directed and self-willed about my chosen path in life, or the plan that I had for what I wanted to do. Sickness can be the salvation of your soul if it becomes an avenue for you to turn away from the course that you've taken and turn to the Lord. If sickness is what brings you closer to the Lord, then it is glorious, not grievous.

The illnesses I've dealt with in my life came in several forms. Sometimes, (and in my case, most of the time) sickness was used as a chastening rod from God. I've often been hard-headed and disobedient to Lord's will! I would get into trouble with God because I wanted my will for my life to be His will. I was good at rationalizing how my worldly plans fit into the plan of God.

It has always been my nature to work, work, work and keep going when I have something I'm determined to do. God has blessed me with a tremendous amount of creative energy and I was using it all for my career. No time to think about the Lord because I was working. Couldn't stop and listen to those who were trying to warn me about my chosen course. I had to work! No time for Bible study, church, or Sunday school—too busy working! I had a plane to catch. I had a deadline to meet. I had things to do and I was too busy to stop and to listen! My career was starting to take precedence over everything, including the Lord, my marriage, and my family.

Since sickness is about the only thing that stops me in my tracks, God sent sickness into my life. I couldn't work, travel, write, or do anything because I was flat on my back, sick as a dog! All my grand plans came to a halt. All I could do was meditate and pray. I had plenty of time to examine my life, honestly look at my faults, to think about the Lord, and pray for forgiveness for my disobedience.

With every illness, I've had the opportunity to tap into the power of a healing prayer. My pastor believes in the power of prayer for the sick, and he's often prayed for me. As with everything in this Christian life, healing is in accordance with your faith.

Sometimes, my faith wavered in the face of the sickness I was dealing with at the time. I begin to feel sorry for myself and fell into that old self pity mantra of "why me?" Why me, Lord when others are doing things that are so much worse? Why me, Lord when I've been trying to serve you? The answer I found is because God loves me, that's why.

Sickness has brought me closer to Him, provided an opportunity for me to exercise my faith, and shown me the power of the Lord working in His people through the prayers of my pastor and my church family.

I've had other illnesses and ailments that were for the glory of God. I once had a physical ailment that baffled my doctors. I was given medicines for my condition that just didn't work. I've been at wits end with my health, but every time I've mustered up enough faith to ask for healing, God has blessed me.

I've learned to glorify God when He miraculously delivers me from sickness and heals me. I've also learned to glorify the Lord if He chooses to leave me in the physical state that I'm in. I've found that if I have faith, He will give me the strength to do His will, no matter what condition my health might be in.

I've also been emotionally sick from the poisons of bitterness and anger. Before I became a Christian, I didn't just have emotional baggage, I had a moving van packed full of every hurt, unkind word, or bad experience I had ever gone through. I had an emotional DVD player set on repeat in my mind that replayed the hurtful incidents over and over and over again. I've been in a depressed state of mind that had me listless, without energy, sad, and miserable. I've had to learn how to pray for my emotional health and to ask for prayer so that I could move past the pain. By the grace of God, I am healed today—mentally, physically, and spiritually.

The illnesses I've been through have all been a test of my faith, and my belief in the healing power of God. It's so easy to say that you know that God can heal and all power is in His hands. But when your health fails, and you're so ill that you can't get out of bed, or when the doctor tells you have some type of terrible ailment, that is when your faith is put to the test. Sickness often determines what you truly believe about the working power of God.

When you're sick, don't look at it as an evil thing that has befallen you. Look at sickness as a blessing from God. Don't get caught up in the mindset that a blessing only comes in the form of something tangible. Sickness is a blessing from God when it is viewed through the eyes of faith.

I no longer ask the Lord "why me?" Why not me? He knows that through the trials I've been through with my health that I've learned to glorify Him. He knows that I've grown in my faith and each and every miracle that He has performed in my life has drawn me closer to Him. He knows that I will testify about His healing power. He knows all about me, and He knows all about you and what you're going through.

If you're ill, take this time to examine your life, draw closer to the Lord, truly repent, pray, and grow in your faith. Miracles aren't a thing of the past. I'm a walking miracle and you can be a walking miracle, too, if you have the faith to believe that God can heal you.

COMMENTS BY PASTOR SALEM ROBINSON, JR.

As a Christian, exactly how can I get authority over sickness in my life and claim a more victorious life in Christ? We can turn to the Bible for an answer to this question.

> Is any among you afflicted? let him pray. Is any merry? let him sing psalms. Is any sick among you? let him call for the elders of the church; and let them pray over him, anointing him with oil in the name of the Lord: And the prayer of faith shall save the sick, and the Lord shall raise him up; and if he have committed sins, they shall be forgiven him. Confess your faults one to another, and pray one for another, that ye may be healed. The effectual fervent prayer of a righteous man availeth much. *James 5:13–16*

The dread of sickness and disease has caused many to seek healing only to find disappointment and despair at the hands of unscrupulous charlatans. Health, happiness, and success have always been three of the most sought after jewels of life. Even when given a hypothetical choice of the trio, good health stands alone as the most important and essential to life. With all the medical breakthroughs of the 21st century, still we are left knowing that healing can only come outside of our wisdom and abilities. The sobering truth is that sometimes even doctors can't heal! Just like farmers having no qualms about admitting their bounty of crops are solely dependent on God's favor and mercy; we must surmise as well that healing is only possible through the tender care of God.

How God Uses an Illness to His Glory

One of the most sobering teachings of Jesus is found in John:

> And as Jesus passed by, he saw a man which was blind
> from his birth. And his disciples asked him, saying,
> Master, who did sin, this man, or his parents, that he
> was born blind? Jesus answered, Neither hath this man
> sinned, nor his parents: but that the works of God
> should be made manifest in him. *John 9:1–3*

This passage teaches us that the human spirit must be challenged to avoid conventional judgmental thinking. We have been conditioned to think that all sickness should be interpreted as evil and that someone has to be blamed for its existence. To accept that the presence of sickness can be allowed of God for the sole purpose of giving glory to God is definitely a paradigm shift. To view sickness as an agent of God as opposed to an agent of Satan to buffet us, definitely stimulates intellectual and spiritual reasoning.

In our sickness, God may be speaking to us or through us. I agree that sometimes it is quite difficult to discern through this paradoxical dilemma of exactly what role a particular sickness is playing in our lives. How we respond to sickness reveals our true belief in God's promise. The Bible reminds us:

> And we know that all things work together for good to
> them that love God, to them who are the called according to his purpose. *Rom. 8:28*

Again, examine this revolutionary concept that something good can emerge out of something seemingly bad.

God's Authority over Sickness

The church is not living up to its potential in exercising authority over sickness, disease, and even satanic forces. We have to submit ourselves to God, resisting the devil, before he will flee from us. As Christians, we must submit first to the authority of obedience to God before we can expect to execute any authority over sickness, disease, and Satan. While we try to exercise authority over these forces, we live lives that do not reflect the authority of God over us. When we respect the divine authority of God that He places over us, we will begin to see our authority over sickness, disease, and evil increase in our lives. We need to understand the flow of authority!

> Then he called his twelve disciples together, and gave them power and authority over all devils, and to cure diseases. *Luke 9:1*

GAINING POWER OVER SICKNESS

> I am the vine, ye are the branches: He that abideth in me, and I in him, the same bringeth forth much fruit: for without me ye can do nothing. If a man abide not in me, he is cast forth as a branch, and is withered; and men gather them, and cast them into the fire, and they are burned. If ye abide in me, and my words abide in you, ye shall ask what ye will, and it shall be done unto you. *John 15:5–7*

In this passage, Jesus is showing us the mystery and the keys to gaining power over sickness. He says it's all about respecting authority—His authority!

Christ states that if you want healing, bring your body, soul, and spirit under subjection to Him and He will give you His power. Keep in mind that Jesus declared that, "all power is given unto me in heaven and in earth," (Matt. 28:18). Sicknesses, whether they be physical, emotional, or spiritual, are mere spirits that tremble at the authority of Jesus Christ. Strive lawfully at His word, claim His authority through obedience, and then wait for the revealed purpose for your sickness.

> Not that I speak in respect of want: for I have learned, in whatsoever state I am, therewith to be content. *Phil. 4:11*

Paul learned this valuable lesson as well:

> And lest I should be exalted above measure through the abundance of the revelations, there was given to me a thorn in the flesh, the messenger of Satan to buffet me, lest I should be exalted above measure. For this thing I besought the Lord thrice, that it might depart from me. And he said unto me, My grace is sufficient for thee: for my strength is made perfect in weakness. Most gladly therefore will I rather glory in my infirmities, that the power of Christ may rest upon me. *2 Cor. 12:7–9*

The life of the Apostle Paul reveals to us how to handle sickness in the life of a believer. Paul was convinced that his sickness was a hindrance to the work of God. He sought God to remove it from his flesh three times, but to no avail. The scriptures tell us that after learning the purpose of his sickness, this man of God accepts God's will over his will and then presses forward to accomplish his calling.

Imagine genuinely accepting that sickness is a blessing from God! God's answer to Paul's prayer to remove his sickness was to trust Him at His wisdom and purpose concerning Paul's sickness and focus on the grace that was given him to accomplish His will. What a profound awakening about how to deal with sickness and healings!

THE MIRACULOUS POWER OF FAITH

Did you know that Jesus refused to do miracles where the people did not have the faith to believe?

And he did not many mighty works there because of their unbelief. *Matt. 13:58*

This father, seeking out Jesus for relief for his disturbed son, is confronted with his own demon of unbelief. His struggles play a huge role in receiving help for his son.

And he asked his father, How long is it ago since this came unto him? And he said, Of a child. And ofttimes it hath cast him into the fire, and into the waters, to destroy him: but if thou canst do any thing, have compassion on us, and help us. Jesus said unto him, If thou canst believe, all things are possible to him that believeth. And straightway the father of the child cried out, and said with tears, Lord, I believe; help thou mine unbelief. *Mark 9:21–24*

The requirement for miracles today has not changed—faith is still the necessary ingredient. Every time we board an aircraft, step onto a ship, or sit behind the wheel of an automobile, we have confidence and an expectation that we will arrive at our destination. I have yet to hear someone ask a flight attendant if parachutes were available. The thought that we might fail to make it to our desired destination is not even entertained as an option. What if we used this type of faith when it comes to receiving healing from God?

As Christians, we must have the faith that all things work together for good to them that love God. That means that whatever we have to go through in this life is ordained and sanctioned by God. Whether in sickness or in health, we endure all without the loss of faith—trusting that God has a higher calling and purpose that sometimes eludes even our understanding.

Pastor Robinson's Sunday School Lesson

Are You Ready for a Miracle?

What's keeping you from your miracle? If we are tempted, God is able to deliver us from temptation. If we are sick, He is able to heal. And whenever we need a miracle, God is still a miracle worker! It seems that many times the reason why we fail to receive an answer from God today is not because we have not prayed, or because we don't know the way or the will of God, it's because of a lack of faith!

Faith is putting your weight upon the faithfulness of God. It is a natural response to the evidence of the true existence of God in your life. Pretending to lean on God is one thing, but you will never really put your full weight on an imaginary support. Consider the following verses:

John 2:3–5, 11

3 And when they wanted wine, the mother of Jesus saith unto him, They have no wine.

4 Jesus saith unto her, Woman, what have I to do with thee? mine hour is not yet come.

5 His mother saith unto the servants, Whatsoever he saith unto you, do it.

11 This beginning of miracles did Jesus in Cana of Galilee, and manifested forth his glory; and his disciples believed on him.

Mary directed them to observe his orders without disputing, or asking questions. Are you really ready for a miracle? Can you be that obedient?

Mark 10:46–52

46 And they came to Jericho: and as he went out of Jericho with his disciples and a great number of people, blind Bartimaeus, the son of Timaeus, sat by the highway side begging.

47 And when he heard that it was Jesus of Nazareth, he began to cry out, and say, Jesus, thou son of David, have mercy on me.

48 And many charged him that he should hold his peace: but he cried the more a great deal, Thou son of David, have mercy on me.

49 And Jesus stood still, and commanded him to be called And they call the blind man, saying unto him, Be of good comfort, rise; he calleth thee.

50 And he, casting away his garment, rose, and came to Jesus.

51 And Jesus answered and said unto him, What wilt thou that I should do unto thee? The blind man said unto him, Lord, that I might receive my sight.

52 And Jesus said unto him, Go thy way; thy faith hath made thee whole. And immediately he received his sight, and followed Jesus in the way.

Mark 1:40–42

40 And there came a leper to him, beseeching him, and kneeling down to him, and saying unto him, If thou wilt, thou canst make me clean.

41 And Jesus, moved with compassion, put forth his hand, and touched him, and saith unto him, I will; be thou clean.

42 And as soon as he had spoken, immediately the leprosy departed from him, and he was cleansed.

Judg. 6:13–15

13 And Gideon said unto him, Oh my Lord, if the Lord be with

us, why then is all this befallen us? and where be all his miracles which our fathers told us of, saying, Did not the Lord bring us up from Egypt? but now the Lord hath forsaken us, and delivered us into the hands of the Midianites.

14 And the Lord looked upon him, and said, Go in this thy might, and thou shalt save Israel from the hand of the Midianites: have not I sent thee?

15 And he said unto him, Oh my Lord, wherewith shall I save Israel? behold, my family is poor in Manasseh, and I am the least in my father's house.

Luke 23:8

8 And when Herod saw Jesus, he was exceeding glad: for he was desirous to see him of a long season, because he had heard many things of him; and he hoped to have seen some miracle done by him.

Neither Herod nor Pilate were ready for a miracle. A genuine miracle will generate more than a superficial or temporary interest. It will have an abiding effect. Miracles are not for your entertainment or amusement.

John 6: 26

26 Jesus answered them and said, Verily, verily, I say unto you, Ye seek me, not because ye saw the miracles, but because ye did eat of the loaves, and were filled.

A LIVING MIRACLE!

DEACON DAVID OSHOKO, SR.

I never would have imagined that I would be living in a world where there are so many people that do not believe in miracles. Many of these same people claim to have faith in God. If there are no miracles, then why is it that I am still alive after having a serious brain surgery operation at the age of 42?

My name is David Oshoko and I am only one of God's many living miracles. I'm originally from Lagos, Nigeria. I came to this country in 1982 to further my education. I was determined to be successful in life and obtained a degree in business agriculture. From Atlanta, Georgia, I moved to the small town of Tifton where I attended Abraham Baldwin Agricultural College for a year before transferring to Southwest Texas State University (now Texas State University) in San Marcos, Texas.

After I graduated, it seemed that my lifelong dreams were becoming reality, but deep inside, my life was truly empty. I tried to fill the void in my heart by drinking and partying and had what many say was a good time. It was not until I accepted Jesus Christ as my personal savior that I finally understood what peace with God was all about. I knew that the Lord had performed a miracle by changing the entire course of my life. What I didn't know was that His plan included taking me to death's door in order to increase my faith. My illness also caused others to consider the miraculous power of God.

I had gone to Ghana with a church group for a missionary trip. I had intended to go home for a visit to Lagos after it was over. One afternoon, I began to feel very weak and decided to rest. No one had any idea as to what was wrong with me. My body went into a seizure. It was decided that I would be rushed back to my home in Austin, Texas for treatment. The doctor took x-rays and showed me that I had a brain tumor the size of a golf ball. The x-ray results could not identify if the tumor was cancerous, but the tumor needed to be removed as soon as possible. The doctor told me that if the operation was not performed soon, that I would die. I was scheduled for surgery a week and a half later.

Although I wasn't in a lot of pain, the doctor said that I had had this tumor for a long time. The only noticeable symptoms were headaches, sinus problems, and when I was asleep, my body would sometimes shake uncontrollably. I found out later that these symptoms were caused by the pressure of the tumor growing in the brain.

Although my doctor said that he felt that I had a good chance of surviving my surgery, I could possibly have diminished memory and nervous system abnormalities, and possibly cancer. He also said that I would be under a doctor's supervision for the next five years to ensure that the tumor didn't return. He told me that after this type of surgery, it often takes years before people feel close to the way that they felt before the surgery.

I went to my pastor's house for him to pray for me before the surgery. Pastor Robinson also came to the hospital the day of the surgery and stayed throughout my surgery. In order to get to the tumor, the doctors had to cut through my skull from my left ear to my right ear. The surgery took about 10 hours. I knew that God was able to heal me from this tumor and that He could make me whole again.

Immediately after the surgery, the first words I said were, "Let's pray." Pastor Robinson prayed for me and I went back to sleep. Later, when I woke up, I asked for a hamburger and a milkshake! After staying in the hospital for about a week, I had to learn to walk again. The test results showed that my tumor was benign. It took about 3 months to recover enough to go back to work. The doctors told me that they were surprised that I had improved so quickly. I went in for yearly visits to check on my progress. I was supposed to visit each year for the next five years. Because of my rapid recovery, I was told no further check-ups were necessary. The doctors said they had never seen anyone recover so fast from this type of surgery! Right there, I had to give God the glory.

I've learned that you must have faith in the Lord so that when you go through a trial of your faith, you can hear what God is trying to say to you. I know that we serve a mighty God and that He is a God of second chances. I know that only God can heal and that you cannot put all your faith in doctors. I also know that "the prayer of a righteous man availeth much..." (James 5:16).

I thank God for my wife, Lutrecia, who stood by me during that time. A Christian woman who loves God will always stand by her husband. She did a lot to take special care of me. Everyone that I have told about my brain surgery is amazed by the fact that I had such a rapid and complete recovery.

I realize that we are all in a spiritual race and the God that we serve is real. The miracle of my recovery after my surgery has made me trust God even more. No matter what I'm going through, I can always depend on God and I trust Him.

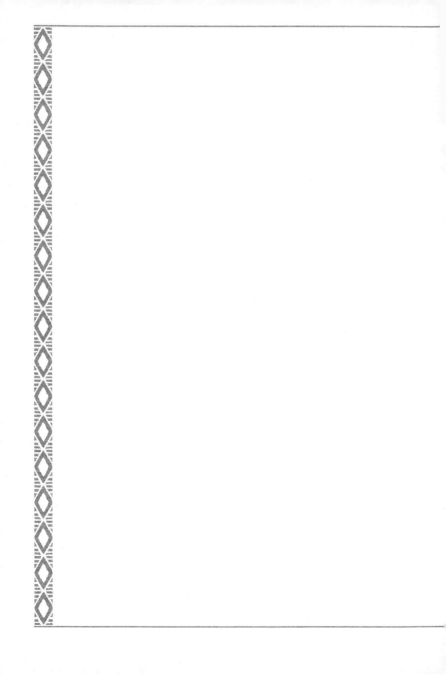

Chapter Six: Friendship
ANGELA'S TESTIMONY

Before I became a Christian, God's definition of a friend and my definition were completely different. I wanted to have lots of friends, but I've learned the hard way that true friendship is something that only happens when both people have the love of God in their hearts. Any other type of relationship is just an acquaintance. Having an acquaintance, a causal relationship, or a so-called friendship with a sinner can never be built on trust because they never reveal their true selves to you. The freedom to live honestly and to be yourself and the knowledge of how to be a true friend only comes when you accept Jesus Christ.

This is not to say that there aren't misunderstandings among Christian friends, but the spirit of Christ gives you the power to love, forgive, and forbear with others, and that includes your friends. A Christian friendship is based on the love of God and honesty. I seek friendships and fellowship with Christians who share my desire to grow in the Lord and serve Him out of a pure heart. My friends tell me the truth in a loving way, support me, encourage me, and yes, go shopping and socialize with me like friends often do.

I've been friends with the same group of Christians for more than 30 years! They've loved and prayed with me through numerous ups and downs, and I've done the same for them. I've also made new Christian friends, and even though we've only known each other for a short time, because we share the same beliefs, I have that same comfort level with them. Christ is the common denominator in a Christian friendship, and that divine love is what makes the relationship so special.

If a person you're calling your friend is a sinner, or claims to be a Christian, but only has a sporadic relationship with God, they can't be trusted to treat you with a real love, either. When you and your friend both have a true love for God, you'll be obedient to His commandments about love. That same godly love will overflow into every relationship, especially your friendships.

The love of God will ensure that your friend will never do the treacherous, hurtful, or underhanded things so-called "friends" have done to each other that I so often hear about. I'm puzzled by Christians that continue to maintain these "friendships" after their "friend" continues to demonstrate in every way possible that they don't really love or care about them. Once you see the true nature of a person and it is hurtful, dishonest, and evil, move on, get them out of your life, and seek out friends that love God out of a pure heart.

I've learned that your friends matter to God. You can't be unequally yoked with a non-believer in a marriage and the same is true in a friendship. You'll always be pulling against each other. A Christian will try to get a sinner to do the right thing and a sinner will try to get a Christian to do the wrong thing.

Who do you invite when you're throwing yourself a pity party? The old saying "misery loves company" is true. If you surround yourself with people that press you down instead of lifting you up, you'll never experience the joy of life.

I've heard Christians use the excuse that they continue to maintain daily contact and a close association with sinners because "they're trying to win them to Christ." In reality, your sinner friend will know that you've changed and truly accepted Christ because you'll refuse to do the things that you used to do.

If you are truly living for Christ, your sinner friends will notice that your lifestyle and your conversation have changed. They'll know that you're born again because you'll no longer party, drink, smoke, chase after the opposite sex, sleep around, do drugs, gossip, lie, gamble, cheat, or any number of other sinful things that you used to do with them before accepting Christ. Talk is cheap. Your new life in Christ will testify for you.

If your so-called sinner friends keep contacting you, all you have to do is politely refuse to go with them anywhere or to carry on an inappropriate conversation. You just say "no" to the sin in their lives and "yes" to the Christ in your own life. If you politely tell them that their cursing is disrespectful to you and that you'd appreciate it if they didn't say vulgar things, they'll get the message loud and clear that you've changed.

If all you talk about is your new life in Christ, how you're improving yourself with the help of the Lord, and about how you feel at peace for the first time in your life, the conversation with your old "friend" will either be brief or they will want to know how they can get what you have. Water seeks its own level. Once they realize that you've risen to a much higher level, they'll start looking for someone who makes them feel comfortable in their sins or they'll ask you how to find Christ.

There's no middle ground once you become a Christian, you'll either win your sinner friends to Christ or they will overthrow your faith and encourage you to go back into your old sins. One thing I've noticed: when a sinner convinces a Christian to leave the Lord and go back into their sins, the sinner often abandons them just the way that person abandoned Christ.

As a Christian, you have to take a stand for what is right, especially when it comes to your family and your old friends. If you truly have a new life in Christ, the love you show to your family and friends is the way that you live before them.

If you live your life in a way that pleases God, then you can help others to see the error of their ways. The old saying that "a Christian is the only Bible some folks are going to read" is true. If you love your family and your friends, live a life before them that they can hold up as an example of someone who is truly a Christian.

COMMENTS BY PASTOR SALEM ROBINSON, JR.

It could be said that we live in an age of strangers. Very few neighbors meet at the fence anymore for a friendly chat and most folks don't even know the names of their neighbors. With varying work schedules and so many things we need and want to do, there's very little time for family, let alone friends.

We have many acquaintances at work and church that we would call friends. You enjoy their presence for a few hours, but you never see them anywhere except work or church. There is no deep commitment to them, but then, there is very little deep commitment to anyone or anything in our "hurry up" society. These "friends" are really just acquaintances.

It is a widely accepted truth that you can live out a lifetime and never find a true friend. If you took an inventory of those in your company, how many would you classify as your friends? Is it possible that friends are something that are created and not just found? If this is true, what would be the right mixture to produce a life-long friend? Let's explore what a friend is before we can honestly pursue trying to be one.

Determining what a friend is not is a sure way to uncover the true meaning of friendship. First of all, friends do not kiss or have romantic encounters with one another. If you have been having sex, you are not friends, you are lovers! Being guilty of this type of behavior just moved you off of the bus for the Christian ride to heaven! The modern meaning and terminology of the definition of a boyfriend and girlfriend may be socially accepted, but serves only to perpetuate the abuse of the term friend.

Friends do not lie to one another, nor will a friend exploit you to their own advantage. There is a reason why dishonest people don't have any real friends. Their circle of close contacts resembles more of a list of shady acquaintances than friends, even though they may like to refer to them as such.

Friendship in the Bible

> The poor is hated even of his own neighbor: but the rich hath many friends. *Prov. 14:20*

Solomon's observation of friends is from a worldly perspective and should not be confused with godly friends. Money has a gravitational pull to a person who only wants to be acquainted with you. Any one who is lured into your circle for those reasons isn't a friend. Consider other Bible verses about friendship:

> Faithful are the wounds of a friend; but the kisses of an enemy [are] deceitful. *Prov. 27:6*

> Iron sharpeneth iron; so a man sharpeneth the countenance of his friend. *Prov. 27: 17*

Why is it that some people select friends in the same fashion as selecting a pair of shoes for an occasion? You have one type of friend that accompanies you to the movies; another for going shopping, another for gossiping, and another that you share your intimate secrets with. Talk about musical chairs! But what happens when you get confused about the proper roles of your friends, and your most intimate secret is told to the gossiper? Immediately, friendship becomes overrated.

You must determine which of the "friend" characteristics you desire the most in your life. Finding that one person that you can trust, that loves you for who you are, and who truly has your best interests at heart can be challenging. You can always depend on a friend to tell you the truth and you are always the better for it. So how do you find a friend? To have a friend, you must first be a friend.

A friend loveth at all times, and a brother is born for adversity. *Prov. 17:17*

A TRUE FRIEND

A true friend is always there to listen when you want to just vent, to laugh with you, to cry with you, but above all, will not hesitate to tell you when you're just being contrary to the will of God.

A man that hath friends must shew himself friendly: and there is a friend that sticketh closer than a brother. *Prov. 18:24*

Again, a friend is someone who knows your innermost fears and weaknesses, appears to be your worst critic, but would never compromise the sanctity of your trust. Can you imagine having someone that will stand with you even in hard times, unwavering in their love and support of you?

Therefore all things whatsoever ye would that men should do to you, do ye even so to them: for this is the law and the prophets. *Matt. 7:12*

THE GOLDEN RULE

This rule of reciprocity known as the golden rule is not just the fundamentals of moral fairness but also forms the concepts for basic human rights. The ethics comprising the golden rule will serve as a basis for developing true friendship. Treat people the way that you would want to be treated and watch people respond in a positive way. This self-transformation is essential, not only for finding friends but even in marital relationships. Just like self-centered people may not ever rise above the rank of an acquaintance, self-absorbed people are not suited for holy matrimony.

Christianity isn't a philosophy, it's a daily relationship with God that will empower you to make the necessary changes in your own heart. It's a character flaw to think that your life is much more interesting than those of all the people that you meet. This type of attitude toward others will definitely keep you from making and keeping friends.

Take the time to seek the interests of others before you chime in about your worldviews on life. In order to see and appreciate the value in others, our hearts must reflect a passion for human life and a concern about the feelings of others.

You can choose to be friends with someone and you can choose not to. When people draw strength from you as a person, they want to spend as much time around you as possible. Godly people have a tendency to shy away from negativity, and have an inclination to gravitate to those with uplifting positive attitudes. Friends actually draw strength from one another. When true friends come together they make one another stronger not weaker, this is the reason why your friends matter to God.

PASTOR ROBINSON'S SUNDAY SCHOOL LESSON

Who could possibly have a better friend than Jesus? Jesus Christ is saying that He will be our friend if we are obedient to the command to be a friend to others. If you use the life of Jesus to mirror the walk of a true friend, you won't have a problem being surrounded with godly friends that share your same interests.

Eccles. 4:9–12

9 Two are better than one; because they have a good reward for their labor.

10 For if they fall, the one will lift up his fellow: but woe to him that is alone when he falleth; for he hath not another to help him up.

11 Again, if two lie together, then they have heat: but how can one be warm alone?

12 And if one prevail against him, two shall withstand him; and a threefold cord is not quickly broken.

Luke 11:5–8

5 And he said unto them, Which of you shall have a friend, and shall go unto him at midnight, and say unto him, Friend, lend me three loaves;

6 For a friend of mine in his journey is come to me, and I have nothing to set before him?

7 And he from within shall answer and say, Trouble me not: the door is now shut, and my children are with me in bed; I cannot rise and give thee?

8 I say unto you, Though he will not rise and give him, because he is his friend, yet because of his importunity he will rise and give him as many as he needeth.

John 15:13–14

13 Greater love hath no man than this, that a man lay down his life for his friends.

14 Ye are my friends, if ye do whatsoever I command you.

This type of unselfish servitude epitomizes how to be a friend to another. Laying down one's life has a broader interpretation than offering the ultimate sacrifice in death. You lay down your life when you deny your comfort to bring comfort to others.

Brothers and Sisters in Christ

Sis. Essi Eargle

Sometimes in this life you need to laugh until your stomach hurts.

Sometimes in this life you need to cry until your eyes swell shut, be they tears of joy or pain.

Sometimes in this life you need to smile until your cheekbones hurt.

Sometimes in this life you need to go out of your way to help someone that made you feel like dirt.

In this life we need to sit back and question and compare our actions, and reactions to the word of God and Christ and believe how unworthy we are of eternal life even when we strive with everything in us.

In this life we will have friends, and known and unknown enemies. In life we will have love and sacrifices.

In this life, I am reminded of this love and sacrifice, when I see and am blessed to be in the presence of my Brothers and Sisters in Christ.

In this life, there is nothing more in this present world other than going home to glory that I look forward to more, than coming through Dunn's Memorial church doors and hearing elect Pastor Salem Robinson, Jr. preach about the death, burial, and resurrection of Jesus Christ, the gospel of salvation, heaven, eternity, hell fire, and being delivered from damnation.

In this life, I look forward to hearing the comments of my Brothers and Sisters in Christ, hearing the church say amen, witnessing the testimonies of growth, listening to the stories of my elders in Christ, and hearing my sisters and brothers sing songs that soothe my soul. Receiving needed bear hugs from my sisters and hand shakes and respectful hugs from my brothers.

I am blessed through my Brothers and Sisters in Christ even when every now and then we disagree. In that disagreement by the grace of God a mirror is shined in my direction that challenges my very fibers, and doing better next time, forgiving and forgetting, asking Christ to cleanse my heart, and picking up and moving on. But most encouraging is to know that my brother and my sisters with the same judgment and love for God and Christ are doing and feeling the exact same thing.

Everyday of the week and sometimes in my conscience I can laugh at moments with my Brothers and Sisters in Christ. There is no better life. And I am blessed and grateful for every Sunday School, every Sunday service, every Wednesday night, and every opportunity of fellowship to have Brothers and Sisters in Christ.

Chapter Seven: Single Christian Relationships
ANGELA'S TESTIMONY

'm woefully unqualified to write very much for this chapter on single Christian relationships! My husband, Michael and I got married soon after I accepted Christ. I was only a single Christian for two weeks!

While I don't have any experience as a single Christian, I've had the privilege of observing the lives of several unmarried Christians—from teens to mature adults. It's a beautiful thing to see single people who have devoted their lives and submitted their bodies to Christ. I've been inspired by the lives of those who've provided their testimonies for inclusion in this chapter. I pray that reading about their triumphs in Christ will be uplifting to anyone who is also living a single Christian life.

We live in a time when promiscuity, a lack of self-respect or morals, and living together without the sanction of marriage is accepted, even in most churches! Children are casually born out of wedlock, young people are losing their virginity at younger and younger ages, and sexually transmitted diseases are as rampant in the church as they are in the world. These sins should not be found in the household of faith. I give God the glory that I'm blessed to attend a church where this type of sinful behavior is not tolerated. If the Holy Spirit can't keep you from sin, what is the point of Christianity?

In a time where whorish behavior by both men and women is celebrated, it is uplifting to see examples of single Christians who have committed themselves to a life guided by the commandments of God.

An unmarried Christian who is living by faith has a beautiful testimony of the keeping power of the Holy Spirit. I thank the Lord for my Brothers and Sisters in Christ who are waiting for the Lord to bless them with a mate, and who prove by their lives that greater is He that is in them, than he that is in the world.

COMMENTS BY PASTOR SALEM ROBINSON, JR.

HOW TO HAVE A SINGLE CHRISTIAN RELATIONSHIP

What you see in many examples of so-called "Christian" dating today are really just the practices of the world being adopted by the church. God will not sanction these practices. What I am about to say may be a little hard to digest, but dating (as practiced in the traditional sense today) is not biblical.

The whole approach to secular dating is to present your best self to the other person without revealing your true self, which can be very deceitful. Maybe this is why they call it the 'dating game.' When Christians start the dating process, it can quickly become a great stumbling block to sinners and people of faith. How can Christians really get to know a person of the opposite sex in this modern world and still remain in the will of God?

Single men and women everywhere are looking for their "Mr. and Miss Right." Some single people, including professed Christians, are subscribing and tapping into dating services to exploit those resources for advice and ways to find a soul mate. Has anyone consulted the Bible to see if these same dating rules apply to Christians?

> Flee also youthful lusts: but follow righteousness, faith, charity, peace, with them that call on the Lord out of a pure heart. *2 Tim. 2:22*

As a single Christian, you must be prayerful when pursuing a relationship. I've seen many single Christians enter into the dating game looking for a love connection and end up losing their connection with God.

HOW TO BEGIN A CHRISTIAN RELATIONSHIP

Is the Bible absolute or obsolete? The last time I checked, God's word has not changed and sin has not been redefined. I know that we are in the 21st century, but right and wrong are not relative. My advice to single Christians who are dating is to ask God for an insight to the person that you're interested in. That sounds like a revolutionary concept—actually praying to the Lord for guidance!

First of all, it seems like almost everyone in America claims to be a Christian (when it's convenient), so you should observe a person's walk in Christ for a period of time before showing any type of interest in him or her. Once you are convinced that he or she has a sincere intent to live after godly principles, your intentions to explore a friendship can be made known to that person. Attending a concert, going on a picnic, and sharing time together will give you an insight to the character of the person. I also advise against any physical contact or entertainment that is of any type of sexual nature, especially if attending a movie.

Although it is fine for Christians to have non-Christian acquaintances, friends who are especially close to our heart should be mature believers who are seeking to follow Christ. Something that always baffles me as a pastor is how a woman can be intuitive and discerning as a sinner looking for a mate, but once she becomes a Christian, she pretends that she can't tell when a man has the wrong motives.

A young lady who had recently accepted Christ told me that before she made a profession of faith and became a Christian, she had a very close male friend. I asked her if she had ever kissed this friend. She reluctantly answered, "Yes." I continued, "Did you ever have sex with this person, regardless of who initiated it?" she reluctantly responded, "Yes." I shared with her that any time you have a friend that you have passionately kissed or enjoined in a sexual act, that person is not a friend but a lover.

The first rule of Christian dating is to remove any and all sexual expectations from the relationship. If you want to know a person, and you have aspirations towards a meaningful Christian relationship, you must first seek to be friends.

As Christians, friendship is not awarded, it is earned. This means that you should take your time when getting to know a person and develop an honest friendship. Believe me, pretending to be a friend as well as pretending to be a Christian is like painting over fire-charred wood—eventually it bleeds through the surface.

A CHRISTIAN DATING SCENARIO

I can recall my youngest son, Trey, at the age of about 19, asking me a question about the boundaries for dating as a Christian. He asked me about someone that he was interested in dating, but he didn't want to appear as being too forward. He wanted to know how to let this person know of his interest. This is the classic question concerning the dating dilemma for single Christians.

You see, I raised my boys to respect women and to always be a gentleman. Please bear in mind, that my advice and his own objective, was to remain in godly character while trying to get to know a person of the opposite sex. I told him that it was acceptable to take the direct approach and just honestly tell her that he would like to get to know her better.

I told my son to take his date someplace that was charming, to be decent, and to maintain his Christian character. I told him that if she is impressed with your decency, and saw it as a quality of strength, then you may have someone you might want to pursue a potential relationship with.

If decency and chivalry is not attractive to a woman who is professing to be a Christian, her heart and mind have not comprehended the ways of God. Needless to say, he found someone who saw his love for God and his respect for women as an asset and not a liability. He is now happily married and out of the dating game.

The same dating boundary issues that my son was concerned about should be respected by single Christian adults.

CHRISTIAN DATING AMONG CHURCH MEMBERS

Extra precaution should be taken if you are intending to date a member of the same congregation. Depending on the size of the congregation and the involvement of your pastor, godly counsel should be sought before moving too fast into a new relationship. It should be understood from the very beginning that the two of you are getting to know one another and that there are no guarantees or absolutes in this venture.

Sometimes, when Christians are dating within the church, some weak members of the congregation may have a cruel judgment about the relationship. Therefore, you have to be extra careful not to be a stumbling block before them and conduct yourself with Christian integrity.

MAINTAINING CHRISTIAN INTEGRITY WHILE DATING

As a pastor, my advice to singles entering into the dating scene is to uphold Christian integrity above all things. Remember, it is more important to be compatible spiritually rather than sexually, because the latter can only be discovered after entering into a Christian marriage.

Precursors to sex such as kissing on the mouth should not be a part of the dating process between Christians. Even holding hands should be postponed until later in the relationship.

By maintaining Christian boundaries, we're avoiding a shipwreck and the temptation of crossing over to the point of no return. Hopefully, during the dating process, you will discover each other's true character, unique traits, and differences. You need to ask yourself early in the relationship if you can live with those differences. Sometimes, there is baggage that was not checked in at the gate when you made a profession of faith and neither of you are ready to part with it now. A person can alter their traits or behavior for short periods of time, but they will never conform to your expectations of a Christian mate if they haven't made a true commitment to Christ first.

Did you know that godly carefulness and pureness of conscience would dictate that two single Christians who are dating should never be seen alone at one another's home? Your home is your sanctuary and is off limits while you're dating. That's right, as a Christian you should not be the guest at one another's home without a chaperone.

This may sound old-fashioned, but it is quite necessary when you are trying to be friends first. Who's to say that this initial friendship will escalate to the level of a serious, intimate relationship? This is why it is so important to get to know a person on a deeper, spiritual level before marriage, rather than to try to continue your fact finding mission after you say 'I do.'

Have you noticed when you get the new car fever and your mind is made up to buy a new car, you start finding fault in your old car every time you drive it? Likewise, when you realize that a Christian relationship isn't what you expected, you need to redefine the relationship or terminate it. You both civilly agree to terminate the romantic side of the relationship, while maintaining a Christian friendship, with no ill feelings on either side. Since you've never kissed on the lips, touched each other inappropriately, or entertained each other alone in your home, there's nothing for the skeptics to judge. The next time you see one each other, you can shake hands and greet one another without any condemnation. That's Christian dating!

Any couple who is in a single Christian relationship and who are contemplating marriage should consider long and hard about the love they claim to have for their future spouse. They need to realize that their love must be nurtured and given time to grow. Don't fool yourself—if your future spouse is not committed to loving God, then there is no commitment to loving you.

Pastor Robinson's Sunday School Lesson
Single or Married, Which is Really Better?

 1 Cor. 7:6–15

6 But I speak this by permission, and not of commandment.

7 For I would that all men were even as I myself. But every man hath his proper gift of God, one after this manner, and another after that.

8 I say therefore to the unmarried and widows, it is good for them if they abide even as I.

9 But if they cannot contain, let them marry: for it is better to marry than to burn.

10 And unto the married I command, yet not I, but the Lord, Let not the wife depart from her husband:

11 But and if she depart, let her remain unmarried or be reconciled to her husband: and let not the husband put away his wife.

12 But to the rest speak I, not the Lord: If any brother hath a wife that believeth not, and she be pleased to dwell with him, let him not put her away.

13 And the woman which hath an husband that believeth not, and if he be pleased to dwell with her, let her not leave him.

14 For the unbelieving husband is sanctified by the wife, and the unbelieving wife is sanctified by the husband: else were your children unclean; but now are they holy.

15 But if the unbelieving depart, let him depart. A brother or a sister is not under bondage in such cases: but God hath called us to peace.

Matt. 19:12

9 And I say unto you, Whosoever shall put away his wife, except it be for fornication, and shall marry another, committeth adultery: and whoso marrieth her which is put away doth commit adultery.

10 His disciples say unto him, If the case of the man be so with his wife, it is not good to marry.

11 But he said unto them, All men cannot receive this saying, save they to whom it is given.

12 For there are some eunuchs, which were so born from their mother's womb: and there are some eunuchs, which were made eunuchs of men: and there be eunuchs, which have made themselves eunuchs for the kingdom of heaven's sake. He that is able to receive it, let him receive it.

1 Cor. 7:24–40

24 Brethren, let every man, wherein he is called, therein abide with God.

25 Now concerning virgins I have no commandment of the Lord: yet I give my judgment, as one that hath obtained mercy of the Lord to be faithful.

26 I suppose therefore that this is good for the present distress, I say, that it is good for a man so to be.

27 Art thou bound unto a wife? seek not to be loosed. Art thou loosed from a wife? seek not a wife.

28 But and if thou marry, thou hast not sinned; and if a virgin marry, she hath not sinned. Nevertheless such shall have trouble in the flesh: but I spare you.

29 But this I say, brethren, the time is short: it remaineth, that both they that have wives be as though they had none;

30 And they that weep, as though they wept not; and they that rejoice, as though they rejoiced not; and they that buy, as though they possessed not;

31 And they that use this world, as not abusing it: for the fashion of this world passeth away.

32 But I would have you without carefulness. He that is unmarried careth for the things that belong to the Lord, how he may please the Lord:

33 But he that is married careth for the things that are of the world, how he may please his wife.

34 There is difference also between a wife and a virgin. The unmarried woman careth for the things of the Lord, that she may be holy both in body and in spirit: but she that is married careth for the things of the world, how she may please her husband.

35 And this I speak for your own profit; not that I may cast a snare upon you, but for that which is comely, and that ye may attend upon the Lord without distraction.

36 But if any man think that he behaveth himself uncomely toward his virgin, if she pass the flower of her age, and need so require, let him do what he will, he sinneth not: let them marry.

37 Nevertheless he that standeth stedfast in his heart, having no necessity, but hath power over his own will, and hath so decreed in his heart that he will keep his virgin, doeth well.

38 So then he that giveth her in marriage doeth well; but he that giveth her not in marriage doeth better.

39 The wife is bound by the law as long as her husband liveth; but if her husband be dead, she is at liberty to be married to whom she will; only in the Lord.

40 But she is happier if she so abide, after my judgment: and I think also that I have the Spirit of God.

Rom. 7:1–3

1 Know ye not, brethren, (for I speak to them that know the law,) how that the law hath dominion over a man as long as he liveth?

2 For the woman which hath a husband is bound by the law to her husband so long as he liveth; but if the husband be dead, she is loosed from the law of her husband.

3 So then if, while her husband liveth, she be married to another man, she shall be called an adulteress: but if her husband be dead, she is free from that law; so that she is no adulteress, though she be married to another man.

A Single Male Christian in High School

Bro. David Oshoko, Jr.

As a young child, I accepted Christ after being influenced by some of my peers that made the same choice. I didn't fully understand the life-changing decision I had made to serve the Lord; how to live a clean life on the inside as well as the outside; how to make choices based on the word of God; or most importantly, how to have a clean mind and heart.

I wasn't living the life I was supposed to live, I was just pretending. I was going down a path of destruction, living my life just the way a sinner would even though I claimed that I was a Christian. I was doing things to satisfy my flesh, lying all the time, and always fighting. I wanted to live like a gangster, so I joined a gang, fought, cursed, gambled, and bet.

Then, once I entered into the second semester of my ninth grade year, I became convicted. I repented of all my past sins with the help of my pastor. His purging, his prayers, and his example of how a real Christian should live, has helped me on my Christian journey.

Now that I'm in high school, there are a lot of struggles and temptations when I'm dealing with my classmates and other people at school. One of my problems with my classmates is that they curse too much and it's so disrespectful to somebody who is trying to live a clean and decent life. When I hear them cursing, it clouds my mind. I've come to realize that if they don't respect me enough to stop, then I don't need to be around them.

There's no point in giving up my faith to be around a lot of people who want nothing to do with God. I just thank the Lord for showing me mercy and forgiving me, and for letting me be associated with a wonderful pastor who will take a stand no matter what, and who has helped me deal with my sins.

A SINGLE FEMALE CHRISTIAN IN HIGH SCHOOL

SIS. ANYSA MEDEARIS-BAILEY

I made a profession of faith when I was nine years old. I accepted Jesus as my Savior and confessed that He died for my sins. I'm blessed to be part of a family that loves the Lord, and to have a single, Christian mother, who sets an example for me.

It has been difficult at times being a Christian teenager and keeping my lust under control. I see teens everyday in relationships that are going too fast. At my church, I've learned that teens are too young to date. Dating is for adults to have the opportunity to get to know one another, in a non-lustful fashion. My mother told me something helpful to think about whenever dating crosses my mind, "dating is for people who are ready to get married."

I know that you're probably thinking that I'm a miserable teenaged girl locked deep in a room, or that my beliefs are like being in a straight jacket. You may be saying "being a Christian as a teenager sounds horrible." Well you're wrong. I have fun being a Christian. I enjoy my life. I like going to amusement parks with my church family, going rowing on the lake with my mother and my friends, and going to the movies. I have lots of friends (yes the non-imaginary kind).

I became a Christian because I wanted to become a better person and I didn't want to miss out on creating a special relationship with the Lord. Christ has helped me grow mentally and spiritually and overcome all of my trials. I know that if I continue my life in Christ, that there are more blessings to come.

A Single Christian in College

Sis. Kerissa Mitchell

As a young child having grown up in the church, I thought Christianity was about getting older, getting married, and having children. I told myself that when I was finished having my "fun" in the world, I would get my life together and serve the Lord. Ignorantly, I didn't realize that when the Lord has a plan for your life it may not align with what you want to do.

As a young teenager, my life was consumed with the lust of the flesh, lust of the eye, and the pride of life, or to sum it all up, BOYS! As a sinner, I didn't have the confidence in myself to say what I would or wouldn't do, because the devil was the ruler of my heart and conscience.

On August 20, 2007, I was given a space to repent for all the wrong I had done in my life. I freely surrendered my heart, mind, will, body, and soul to the Lord and have not looked back to the world since that day.

The sinful road I was traveling on before I got saved was going to result in having a baby out of wedlock, or in acquiring some type of incurable disease. I know that the Lord and His mercy prevented any of those things from happening, even when I was a sinner.

For many of my 21 year-old peers, this is their "prime time." This is their time to legally drink, experiment with different things, and to be promiscuous. I'm always reminded of how the Lord has changed my life, and how I've made the right decision to refrain from entering into a Christian relationship until I'm finished with college.

I remember a sermon that my pastor preached entitled "Is It Better To Be Single Or Married?" Of course, the carnal side of the mind says that it's better to be married, but through this sermon, the Lord revealed to me that being single is better.

You may ask why I think that being single is better. I've found that as a single Christian, one has time to build a personal relationship with the Lord. Being single gives me an opportunity to grow in my faith and to mature into a Christian young lady. A single Christian has time to explore what it takes to live this life, and grow in godly wisdom without the distractions of a spouse. As a single Christian young lady, I am learning so many things about Christianity and how to be an example to others. Over the past year, I've become aware of a lot of things about myself. Being a Christian is something that I would never compromise because there is nothing in the world that has brought me greater joy.

When I go to college, I hold in my heart the personal lessons that I have learned about abstaining from the appearance of evil. I don't define my life as being a single Christian young lady. I just look at myself as a Christian.

As a Christian, there are things that I cannot and will not do because all things are lawful, but not all things are expedient. Pastor Robinson has taught me that people are always watching my life and that I have to be a light in this world of darkness. With this godly knowledge, and the new life that the Lord has allowed me to live, I'm the complete opposite of the way I used to be.

A Single Christian Parent

Sis. Deanna Medearis

I used to be your typical, worldly single woman before I became a Christian. I attended church, but I didn't have a real relationship with Christ. I was just a religious person who acted just like sinners did, but somehow felt I was better off than they were because I went to church. I dated, and even though I knew actual sex was off limits, there was little else I refrained from. I told myself that because I didn't have sex and because I attended church, I wasn't that bad. Nothing could have been further from the truth.

On January 12, 2007, I began a new relationship. This relationship was unlike any other relationship I had previously experienced, because this relationship was with Christ. I had never repented of my sins and I finally made a decision to stop being a hypocrite. My life has not been the same since that day. Whereas before, all manner of immoral actions with the opposite sex was both expected and accepted when I went out on a date, my new relationship with Christ required cleanliness of mind, heart, and body. This relationship demanded that the old me die and a new me emerge, and that I lean on God and Christ for my strength.

I have been so blessed since entering into my relationship with Christ. I've learned how to carry myself as a clean, Christian young lady, how to be honest with myself and with others, and how to rely upon prayer and the prayers of my pastor to get me through the tough times. It is a beautiful thing to be able to look at myself in the mirror every morning and not be ashamed of things I did the night before.

I thank God through His Son, Jesus Christ, for my new life. Each day, as I grow in my relationship in Christ, I learn more about Him and consequently, more about myself. I hope and pray that you, too, will understand how necessary it is for those of us who profess to be single Christians to take a stand for purity and not betray the wonderful gift of salvation that we have been given.

How the Lord Blessed Me as a Single Christian Parent

Sis. Diane Nunn

I was raised in the church and I considered myself a Christian even though I was having sex and had a baby out of wedlock. Even with all of the sinful things that I was doing, I still kept my position as secretary of the Sunday School, youth director, and continued to sing in the choir. I was religious and lost, but I didn't know how to live any better at that time.

In 1975, I was invited to attend a small church by some friends. I attended for several months. The minister and the members of the congregation would talk about "counting up the cost to follow Christ." Even though I had been attending a denominational church all of my life, I had never heard of this. So at the age of 25 years old, and completely by faith, I counted up the cost to follow Christ in the hopes of a better life and a new beginning.

I got married a few months later and I thought I had arrived. But after being married for almost five years, my husband decided he no longer wanted to be a Christian. Once again I was looking for a new beginning. I left him and moved in with a friend, and my daughter went to live with the family of a friend so she could continue in school. The first night that I spent alone was like a war in my mind and in my spirit. The bed was literally wet with sweat from wrestling with the troubled thoughts that were in my mind.

During the daytime, my life was pretty normal and routine. Go to work, attend church activities, check on my daughter, and occasionally, visit some of the other single sisters in the congregation. But at night, I had very little peace or sleep. The devil would tell me "you changed your life, but what good has it done you? Look at you! You're still alone and unloved by a man. You're no better off than before. Give it up and go back to your family, your old church, and your old friends." The devil was always present, trying to see if I had truly counted up the cost. But through it all, the Holy Spirit would always be present to bring to my remembrance this scripture:

> For if we sin willfully after that we have received the knowledge of the truth, there remaineth no more sacrifice for sins, but a certain fearful looking for of judgment and fiery indignation, which shall devour the adversaries. *Heb. 10:26–27*

Finally, I accepted the Lord's will for my life as a single Christian woman. I became determined, with help of the Lord, to make a full commitment to Christ and to refrain from getting married again until my daughter was married. I wanted to set a better example as a Christian mother, and I didn't want to subject her to any more emotional upheaval in her life. Once I made that commitment, I could feel the yoke getting easier to bear through the empowerment of the Holy Spirit.

One day, the Spirit told me to buy a new home so I could be reunited with my daughter. No more paying rent, or living separately. I could feel the presence of God every step of the way. About a year later, we moved into our new home. I give glory to God, and thanks to Jesus Christ, my Savior and the Holy Spirit, my teacher, for reuniting me with my daughter, in a new home for a new beginning, and holy quietness.

On some Saturdays, the church would go out to hold a street ministry, but they didn't allow children to go. I asked God to let my mission be to care for the children of the ministers of the church. Many of the ministers were young and their children ranged in age from a few months to 12 years old. My daughter and her friends would help me take care of the older children and I would take care of the babies and toddlers. When Pastor Robinson and his wife, Patricia, would stop by my home to pick up their children, they were never too tired to stay for a visit. We would read and discuss the scriptures or Pastor Robinson would make up questions from the Bible for us to answer. These biblical teachings always encouraged and inspired us.

Then one day, Pastor Robinson and his wife told me that God had shown them that my daughter, Bardia, needed a father figure in her life. The Robinsons had noticed that all of my daughter's friends had a fatherly influence to guide them and to spend time with them. Bardia was often the only one of her friends who was alone during family events. She was about 12 years old at that time and I was blind to all the things that the devil was presenting to her.

The Robinsons would often pick Bardia up from school, or attend parent-teacher conferences on my behalf because I was working. They would often invite her over for dinner after school, help her with her homework, take her shopping, and bring her along with their family when they went on vacations, just as if she was also their child. It's marvelous to observe the endless love God has given them for her, and now that she's married and has children of her own, for my grandchildren. I am truly grateful to God and Jesus Christ for joining our families together.

I'd lived a single Christian life for about 9 years when temptation entered into my life and this scripture became a reality:

> There hath no temptation taken you but such as is common to man: but God is faithful, who will not suffer you to be tempted above that ye are able; but will with the temptation also make a way to escape, that ye may be able to bear it. *1 Cor. 10:13*

The devil came to tempt me in the form of a tall, nice-looking man. He said he remembered seeing me on campus when we attended the same college. He started visiting the library where I worked regularly. I started praying to God and to Jesus Christ. I knew that this man wasn't interested in a Christian relationship and that this was just a trial of my faith that I needed to overcome. I needed my job, but I wanted to get away from that man and preserve my soul, so I put in for a transfer to another library. Thank the Lord I got another job and that He helped me overcome that temptation.

Not by my might, but by God's spirit, I lived a spotless, single Christian life for nearly ten years. Thank the Lord, I've been married now for over 18 years. Having lived as both a single Christian and as a married Christian woman, I've found out that there are very few differences when you've made up your mind to live for Christ. I must continue to present my body a living sacrifice, purify my heart and mind continuously, and surrender my thoughts to Christ. God must be glorified and Jesus Christ lifted up. Amen and Amen.

Life as a Single Christian Man

Bro. Kilpatric Davidson

In January of 2007, I was traveling for my job when God intervened in my life. I'd positioned myself in the tight confines of the airplane seat after yet another long business trip. I was contemplating the redundancy of New Year's resolutions past, all of which seemed to have found their way on my new list of resolutions—get a new job, make more money this year, settle down, and get closer to God.

I began to prepare myself to return to the mess I called my life that awaited me in Hampton Roads, Virginia. The cabin began to fill up and I realized that I might get a whole row of seating to myself. As the flight attendants prepared the plane for departure, I tried to make the row of seats my bed and stretched my legs out across them. Then, a man and woman made their way down the aisle. I was hoping that they would miraculously find a seat somewhere else. Then, the woman, in a calm voice, said…"Is anyone sitting here?" "No," I retorted as I moved my legs and repositioned myself.

Dangling in the air at about 20,000 feet made me think of those seedlings that you see in the springtime, each one at the mercy of the wind controlling it, each one with a purpose, yet no direction. These thoughts were interrupted by the conversation I was having with the couple sitting beside me. I found myself telling them about my ambitions and the direction that I wanted my life to go in, and how I felt that I was stuck in the place that I was in. The woman's solutions to my problems were simply to jump.

Could I let go of the ledge? What was I jumping into? And who was going to catch me? I jumped into a new life in June 2007 when I packed my things and drove to Austin, Texas. I moved in with the couple I'd met on the plane, Michael and Angela Medearis, and began attending Dunn's Memorial Church with them every Sunday, under the ministry of Pastor Salem Robinson, Jr.

Never had I met someone so dedicated to the saving of souls as Pastor Robinson. He spoke sternly about how the decency and character of a person means everything to God. I had a lack of respect for myself that reverberated in a pain so deep inside me that it couldn't be massaged. That's when the mirror of the word of God was placed in front of me and I began to ask myself, "What does it mean to be a single Christian in a world where it's deemed unpopular and virtually impossible?"

As a single man in sin, I found myself bobbing and weaving in and out of relationships. Some of these relationships were long, some short, some even undefined, but all lacking because I was looking for something in them that I hadn't even found in myself.

One of the first lessons taught to me by Pastor Robinson was the need to have a relationship with Jesus Christ. That was a relationship that was nonexistent in my life at the time. Growing up, I was religious, but lost. I knew Christ as the Son of God, but I never really took the time to seek out who He was as a Savior.

Pastor Robinson also spoke of the core belief of every Christian in the death, burial, and resurrection of Christ—another major point that I managed to elude in my life. Like that seedling dangling in the wind, I found myself at the mercies of the world, making unwise decisions that were detrimental in this life and the hereafter. How could I maintain a meaningful relationship with any woman when all of my life I had neglected the most meaningful relationship of all, the relationship with Christ?

I began to see that God had placed me in a ministry that forced me to take a true look at the man that I am now as a Christian; and one that made me look at the person that I used to be. The Lord also provided me with living examples of the power of a righteous walk in Christ. It made me see things that I had done in the past that the numbness of the world had almost allowed me to forget about. I thank God for repentance, the Holy Spirit, and my new relationship with Jesus Christ. He knocked, and I let Him in.

They say that in life you should never look back. But the truth is that if you never look back, you'll never really conceptualize how far the Lord has brought you. I had enough sense to know that God was working on me, but I didn't really understand why He had placed me in a place where the African-American population was only about 10%. What were my odds of finding a prospective wife now?

Sometimes you have to be stripped out of what you've known and what's familiar to you in order to advance to the next stage of life. Being someone who always thought he was in control of his life, I was reluctant to hand over the steering wheel. Honestly, looking back on some situations I put myself in, I probably could have driven better with my eyes closed!

It takes faith to pry your hands from the steering wheel and to allow Christ to show you the direction to go in your life. Christ was crucified, dead and buried, then was resurrected so that we could have a second chance at life. Faith in that now gives me the strength to resist the sins of fornication and the numerous other sins that I'd committed in the past that were vividly revealed to me while in front of 'the mirror' of the word of God.

Not to say that Satan isn't at every corner planting traps to make you stumble and fall. What has to be remembered is that Satan only has three tools of deception—the lust of the flesh, the lust of the eye, and the pride of life—and he doesn't ever hesitate to use them. As a single man, Satan is quick to plant seeds of mischief that will grow into trees if you're not equally yoked and plow your fields constantly. I'm learning to be mindful where I go, what I watch, and what I thoughts I entertain. And above all else, I know that, through Christ, I'm able to withstand any temptation that may come my way. Christ promised that with any temptation, He would provide a way out. Faith is the key. The more faith I attain, the stronger and better I become.

Today as a single Christian man, I walk, enjoying and appreciating everything around me. Even my prayers are different now. I no longer flood God with needy petitions for material things that I want; failing to give Him thanks for the things I already have. Today, I thank Jesus every day when I rise that I have another chance at life. I thank Him for replenishing in me what other relationships failed to do and sustaining me like no one else would. I thank Him for the rod of reproof, and I thank Him for my extreme newfound joy. I thank Him for the knowledge that being a single Christian man is fully possible, for when you have Christ in your life you will never be alone.

Dating as a Male Christian

Bro. Gary Eargle

I was raised in the church, made a profession of faith, and was baptized at an early age. I was living my life, thinking that I was a Christian, trying to do right in my own power, while influenced by the world. Eventually, I started doing worldly things that I knew were wrong before God. Why? Well, it was because I didn't have a relationship with Jesus Christ. I wasn't filled with the Holy Spirit and it is that spirit that gives one the power to live a godly life. I had a love for God, but in reality, I was just religious.

All that started to change in 2002 when I started going to Dunn's Memorial in Austin, Texas and met Pastor Salem Robinson, Jr. I joined the church as a Christian because I was raised in a church that preached that once you're saved, you're always saved, and that if you failed or "backslid" the Lord would forgive you, if you asked. Looking back, I see that I was mainly given the milk of the word and didn't have it ingrained in me that the Lord could keep you from falling. I had been raised under a defeated Christian mentality.

Through Pastor Robinson's teaching and instruction, I've learned what it means to be a real Christian. On September 12, 2004, I gave my heart and my life to Jesus Christ. Later, I talked to Pastor Robinson and told him that I was lonely and wanted to get married. He told me that he would pray for me.

In the Lord's time, after I discussed it with Pastor Robinson, I started talking to Essi Pinkard, a young lady in the church who was a Christian and a godly woman. Pastor Robinson took the time to counsel and instruct Essi and myself about how Christians should "date," which is very unlike the world's definition of dating. With Pastor Robinson's guidance and instruction, Essi and I started talking in order to get to know one another and become friends. That was step one.

When I told Pastor Robinson that we were friends and that we were ready for the next phase of our relationship, Pastor Robinson brought me back to reality. He told me there was no way that we could have gotten to know each other and become friends in such a short time.

I really thank the Lord for Pastor Robinson and his instruction and his wisdom. While Essi and I were dating, we didn't go over to each other's house or apartment to visit unless someone else was present. Now, this kind of "dating" can only be done with the help of the Holy Spirit. It takes the Holy Spirit to keep lust under control. Essi and I were obedient to Pastor Robinson's instructions and after about two years, we were married. We did not even kiss until we said "I do" on our wedding day.

The world says that you can't be involved in a relationship or date without having sex. I'm here to tell you that with God and with the instruction and guidance from a pastor that is called by God, you can be decent, get to know a member of the opposite sex, and have a relationship with them in a godly way.

Dating as a Female Christian

Sis. Essi Eargle

In a sex-crazed society, people are often amazed to hear that my husband Gary and I got a chance to know each other without kissing, groping one another, or having sex. This is contrary to the world because the world teaches you that you should "test each other out" to see if you are sexually compatible with your mate. What a deception of Satan and a cheat! The world does not let you test out a pair of shoes that you buy from the mall for days and weeks at a time, and then bring them back. The shoes are considered used. How much more the human body?

Before I met the Lord Jesus, there was a time when I behaved just like the rest of the world. I was very unhappy with the perversion and filth in which I was involved. The Lord changed me and delivered me from that sinful life.

My advice to single Christians is to spend as much time as possible with the Lord. While it is a blessing to be married, it is an even greater blessing to have the uninterrupted freedom to spend days and hours with the Lord. The Lord is more than able to keep you and supply all of your needs. I learned that by the grace of God, I could live a celibate life until the Lord was ready to send me a husband. The very first time I kissed my husband was on our wedding day. The first time I intimately kissed and had sex with my husband was on our wedding night.

Our pastor teaches the congregation how to live right in obedience to God. My husband and I, through the guidance and instruction of our pastor, have even been taught how to be holy behind closed doors. I can truly say that what God has created in our marriage is beautiful.

Chapter Eight: Christian Marriage
Angela's Testimony

A s a child, I thought that when I got married, it would be like the movies: wind blowing through my hair, violins playing in the background, my makeup always perfect. I imagined a lovely fire crackling in the fireplace of my beautiful home, gently illuminating the face of my handsome husband as he brought me fabulous gifts. I never saw anyone scrubbing toilets! The movies lied to me! That's why so many marriages fail. They're based on the movies, not on the Bible.

Whenever I'm doing housework (including scrubbing the toilets), or picking up my husband's socks off of the floor, I consider the real meaning of marriage. One thing I've learned: it's not about the socks on the floor. When we first got married, I would nag my husband about his habit of throwing his socks on the floor. It got to be a big point of contention every morning, and a horrible way to start the day. After another argument about his socks on the floor, the socks disappeared. There were no socks on the floor for almost two weeks!

One morning, my husband was getting ready to go to work and he didn't have any clean socks. I looked in the hamper, but there weren't any socks in there and I didn't remember seeing any socks when I did the laundry. Then, he sheepishly opened the drawer of the bedside table and revealed that he had been putting his dirty socks in there to avoid all the fussing in the morning. Even though this happened almost 25 years ago, we still laugh about it. I've learned to look at his quirks as a small price to pay for the company of such a sweet man.

Now, I just pick up his socks every morning without complaint. I also look for his keys, his wallet, his cell phone, or something that he's misplaced at least once a week. Whenever I think about complaining, I focus on all the things that I do that he puts up with. For example, sometimes, I love to eat crunchy snacks in bed. No matter what I do, a few crumbs seem to make their way over to his side. I also snore and wake him up in the middle of the night when I have a fabulous idea for a project. He sits patiently beside me while I watch the cooking and decorating shows that I love.

I was 18 and Michael was 20 when we got married. We grew up together, but more importantly, we've grown together as Christians. He married a girl, and by the grace of God, helped to shape me into a woman. He patiently ate some of the worst meals in the western world until I learned how to cook. I realize now that if he had been critical of my cooking skills, I never would have developed the love I have for all things culinary, or developed the confidence I now have in the kitchen.

Michael supports my dreams no matter how wild or impossible they may sound to others. He puts his money where his mouth is, too. When I wanted to become a writer, he worked two part-time jobs and a fulltime job so I could devote myself to learning my craft and getting my work published.

Someone once asked me how we manage to have such a happy marriage in this day and age. I always say that you have to marry someone who truly has the same heavenly goals that you have. I know we're blessed by God, and I thank Him daily for our relationship. The gratitude I have for God blessing my life spills over into my marriage. I don't take my salvation, my husband, or my marriage for granted. I show appreciation for the sweet things he does for me and he treats me the same way. The biblical teachings we've learned are applied to our daily lives and that has made all the difference in our marriage.

I laugh when I'm asked if we ever argue. Of course we disagree, but we know how to disagree without losing our integrity as Christians. You can't just say anything or do anything in a Christian marriage because you're angry. You also can't let those ill feelings linger.

If we can't resolve an issue, we make an appointment with our pastor so that we can get counseling. We've gotten wonderful counsel throughout our 33 years of marriage, and it has been a blessing.

Since very few adults have ever had the privilege of observing a Christian marriage during their formative, childhood years, most of us don't know how to be married. As Christians, we have to learn how to have marital harmony by studying and applying the word of God to our lives.

I always advise Christian couples to get counseling throughout their marriage instead of just when things hit rock bottom. You're cheating yourself out of the happiness that God intended in a Christian marriage if you don't learn how to have a marriage based on the word of God. That means all of the word of God, including the part that outlines the order of a Christian home.

I had a problem with the whole "the man is the head of the home and the woman is supposed to be under subjection" part of the Bible. After all, I'm part of the generation of women that decided that we really didn't need men anymore. We could take care of ourselves! Here's the problem with that concept—it's not biblical and it doesn't work in a Christian marriage.

The majority of the struggles we've had in our marriage have been tied to my absolute refusal to bring my will under subjection to my husband. I wanted to lead and he refused to follow. I refused to let him manage our money, even though he's far better at it than I am. I stubbornly set up a bank account in my name only, I had my own credit cards, and I promptly ran us into a mountain of debt. We had a "my money, your money" marriage, which means we were divided and doomed for failure if we kept going along that path. We were young and silly and God had mercy on our foolishness.

After all the drama, we realized that we truly love each other and want to stay married. We decided to follow the word of God and let the Bible determine what we should do with our lives and our marriage. That renewed commitment to Christ has made all of the difference in our relationship.

I know now that if a man is truly following the Lord, it's easy for his wife and family to let him lead. When a man knows that you admire his having Christ in his life, and that you trust him to let the Lord lead him in his decisions, he'll prayerfully strive to do everything he can to keep that trust that you have in him.

I've learned that I'm more independent in my marriage then I ever would have been as a single woman. Marriage provided me with the security and freedom I needed to fully explore everything that the Lord wants me to do, while having the love, the wisdom, and the support of my best friend, my husband.

We are joined as one in this relationship and there are many things that I do because those are the talents the Lord has blessed me with. There are other things that Michael has been blessed with the skills to do, and I turn those tasks over to him. He respectfully discusses his decisions with me, and I do the same.

Everything you need to know about how to have a successful marriage is in the Bible. As with everything else on this Christian journey, it isn't hard to do the will of the Lord once you make up your mind that's what you want to do. Many of the conflicts and struggles in a marriage are because we don't want to be obedient to the word of God. The peace and marital harmony my husband and I now have is a direct result of our obedience to God.

A Christian marriage is composed of many different elements—spiritual, emotional, and physical. The physical aspect of a Christian marriage is an important part of that relationship. Unfortunately, many so-called Christian married couples have a "daytime" appearance of holiness, but at night, they lead unholy lives in the bedroom.

As a Christian couple, we have to live a life that is pleasing to God in the light as well as in the dark. The pornographic, unnatural acts that are accepted by the world as the sexual norm are not sanctioned by God. What you do, even in the privacy of your own bedroom, is seen by God.

If you are committing sexual acts with your spouse that condemns your conscience, you need to get counseling and repent. If you're trying to justify the unnatural things you're doing because "you're trying to hold your marriage together," or "nothing we do in the bedroom is wrong because we're married," you're deceiving yourself.

As with everything else we need to know as Christians, we have a perfect example of the way a couple should and should not be intimate outlined in the word of God. There is a biblical way ordained by God for a husband and a wife to be intimate that is a beautiful spiritual and physical connection between two people who love each other. This is a blessed physical union that is sexually and emotionally fulfilling and satisfying and, best of all, it was designed by God. After more than 33 years of marriage, Michael and I can testify that if you adhere to all of the biblical principals pertaining to Christianity, including what you do in the bedroom, your marriage will be a happy one!

A Christian marriage is the earthly example of the relationship that Christ has with the church of God. The sacrifice, devotion, love, care, concern, understanding, patience, misunderstandings, and humorous parts of a marriage all reflect elements of the relationship we have with Christ. As a carpenter friend of ours says "you can't build a 50 story building on sand." The same holds true for a marriage. If the foundation of a marriage is built on Christ, you've got a solid rock to build on for all time.

Comments by Pastor Salem Robinson, Jr.

A Christian marriage is for life. Your marriage vows should have included, "until death do us part." The strength of these marriage vows allows the couple (out of a fear and respect for God) to be more honest with each other: they both know the marriage is for life. A godly marriage is designed this way because a lifelong commitment is needed to force couples to work through their difficulties with each other. Love is about commitment! Without commitment love does not have a chance to grow.

The commitment made to each other when taking the marriage vows should also echo a couple's mutual commitment to living a Christian life. If you want to have marital harmony, both of you must choose to walk a godly path with the same destination: heaven. Your life becomes discordant when your hearts are not knitted together with the same godly purpose. When you walk with God, you will come into harmony with your innermost feelings and challenge the very essence of your self. If both parties in a relationship can shed the shackles of dishonesty and look into their own minds and hearts, you will find rest in your soul and peace in your marriage.

When your soul is content, harmony abounds. This harmony will manifest itself as true love, both within your marriage and with God. Since we are made in the image of God, you will never find peace until you and your spouse both have faith in God.

Occasionally, there are unfortunate circumstances in which a Christian is joined to an unbeliever. This union is not outside the influence of God, but the responsibility is now placed on the child of God to present himself without blame before God and before the unbelieving spouse. Impeccable behavior is a necessity, not only to show the unbelieving spouse the way of God, but to avoid the temptations of sinful desires not sanctioned by God.

And the woman which hath an husband that believeth not, and if he be pleased to dwell with her, let her not leave him. For the unbelieving husband is sanctified by the wife, and the unbelieving wife is sanctified by the husband: else were your children unclean; but now are they holy. But if the unbelieving depart, let him depart. A brother or a sister is not under bondage in such [cases]: but God hath called us to peace. *1 Cor. 7:13–15*

It also happens that husbands and wives find themselves at different levels of spiritual and emotional maturity. It is important to help each other grow and never be condescending to your partner. Intimacy in a marriage will grow when you are able to adjust, not lower, your expectations towards each other.

MY HUSBAND/MY WIFE, MY FRIEND FOR LIFE

If two people share the same path, it is natural for a close friendship to form. At the heart of every healthy marriage is a strong friendship. Marriage is one of the highest levels of the relationships created by God, thus friendship is highly esteemed in the context of the marriage relationship.

Why are friendship and companionship so important? Shared experiences lead to shared feelings. It's unhealthy for a married person to spend the most enjoyable moments of his or her life in the company of someone else. Friends spend time together, have fun together—and grow fonder, not wander! Close friends talk. Marriage counselors say couples not only need to talk, but they that need to talk at least one hour per day.

The things that hold a marriage together are the same binding traits that are esteemed among friends. Think about it—within friendship is trust, respect, genuine compassion, and a love unabated by changing circumstances. Everyone wants not only someone to be married to, but someone who will also be their friend!

Although love can occur naturally between two godly people as their relationship develops and strengthens, the main reason you should love your wife is because God says that you should do so. This may sound strange, but being obedient to the word of God lays a solid foundation for marital harmony and helps a couple weather any future trials in the relationship. Loving your spouse because God tells you to will help to keep your love firm during those immature and silly moments.

Sometimes in a marital relationship, a person may face difficulties that might challenge his or her immature love for their spouse. Many people have even dissolved their marriages because their love was immature. After awhile, you will learn that love has more to do with your obedience to the commitment and the maturing love you have for your spouse than how you feel emotionally during a trying time in your relationship.

THE ROLES OF CHRISTIAN SPOUSES

Accepting gender roles as laid out in the Bible can be difficult for many married couples. However, when looked at closely, they reveal divine wisdom essential for a godly marriage.

> Likewise, ye husbands, dwell with them according to knowledge, giving honour unto the wife, as unto the weaker vessel, and as being heirs together of the grace of life; that your prayers be not hindered. *1 Pet. 3:7*

This is one of the most misunderstood Bible passages about the roles of husbands and wives. The Apostle Peter is simply saying that men and women are different and that these differences must be understood if man and wife are to dwell together in harmony. Peter instructs husbands to show the wisdom of God by first honoring their wives in the greatness that they were created. He then instructs them to apply the knowledge that women are the weaker vessel.

This is where men get into trouble and marital harmony can seem impossible. The Apostle Peter is not saying that women are inferior in any respect, even though they are under subjection to their husbands. This scripture illustrates that women are different than men and harbor different needs and wants. To overlook this could prove fatal in keeping harmony in the home. Peter concluded that the husband's prayers could be hindered if they lack this insight concerning their wives.

It is not demeaning for a godly woman to recognize a godly husband as her spiritual head under Christ. Submission by a wife to her husband means she is recognizing God's plan and authority.

> Wives, submit yourselves unto your own husbands, as it is fit in the Lord. *Col. 3:18*

Biblical submission also means that the wife manifests a deep love and respect toward her husband. It does not mean the wife is relinquishing her personal identity. True submission in a marriage is not enslavement; it is liberation.

> Nevertheless let every one of you in particular so love his wife even as himself; and the wife see that she reverence her husband. *Eph. 5:33*

Now this is how you spell marital harmony—RESPECT! When a man loves his wife just like he would care for himself, the natural response from his wife is reverence; a genuine respect.

A wife is to be glorified and esteemed very highly by her husband. When the husband not only understands this, but practices this within the relationship, and the wife submits herself to her husband, the couple is following the biblical example of a Christian marriage.

Physical Intimacy

Physical intimacy is an important part of a Christian marriage and is part of the physical bond that unites the hearts of a Christian man and woman. However, secular concepts of what is acceptable sexual behavior should not be part of the intimacy shared by married Christians.

As a pastor, I find it alarming to see ungodly and secular views of marriage being shared by professed Christians. I expect a non-Christian to say something ignorant like, "I can't imagine having sex with the same person for the rest of my life," but I don't expect a statement like this from a Christian! If you are a Christian having these thoughts, then you have no real concept of a Christian marriage; in fact, your relationship with Christ is really in question.

Marriage and intimacy are remarkably divine when you have been prepared of God. The Bible says that when you choose marriage, you give authority over your body to your husband and likewise your husband gives authority over his body to you. Since the two of you are joint owners of one another's body, you both have to agree about being or not being intimate.

> Nevertheless, to avoid fornication, let every man have his own wife, and let every woman have her own husband. Let the husband render unto the wife due benevolence: and likewise also the wife unto the husband. The wife hath not power of her own body, but the husband: and likewise also the husband hath not power of his own body, but the wife. *1 Cor. 7: 2–4*

Do you feel that you can reach this level of sharing in a marriage? If this scripture is hard for you to accept, then you may not be ready for marriage. The scriptures are not suggestions but commandments for our lives.

There are times when it is appropriate to practice celibacy. The Bible says it is acceptable to refrain from sex for fasting or prayer. But the Bible also warns of the danger of extended celibacy:

> Defraud ye not one the other, except it be with consent for a time, that ye may give yourselves to fasting and prayer; and come together again, that Satan tempt you not for your incontinency. *1 Cor 7:4–5*

The incontinency referred to in the verse above denotes a lack of restraint that can give way to temptation if you withdraw from one another too long and refrain from being intimate. Your desire to want to be more spiritual by denying sexual gratification is not wrong, but don't try to surpass the saints of biblical times and neglect your marriage duties.

THE NEED FOR COMMUNICATION

If you and your spouse are both living godly lives and share the same Christian goals, but are still experiencing trouble in your relationship, you may not be communicating properly.

> Let no corrupt communication proceed out of your mouth, but that which is good to the use of edifying, that it may minister grace unto the hearers. *Eph. 4:29*

Some couples don't cope well with their problems, and their conversations often turn into fights, so they stop wanting to talk or use words as punishment. How do you control your feelings towards your spouse when you are hurt or distraught? Do you express how angry or disappointed you are without further damaging the relationship? One of the many things that creates a successful marriage is communicating freely yet lovingly with each other whenever problems arise. Each spouse must acknowledge his or her contribution to the problem. You also must take responsibility for how the other feels.

Quarrels are the result of a couple allowing their angry emotions to take control. Verbal strife occurs when a couple refuses to deal with the issues at hand, instead they attack the other personally. Do you try to hurt one another even at the risk of sinning against God? You must maintain a mutual respect for one another even when resolving conflicts. We must learn how to bring our feelings under subjection to God.

> For the wrath of man worketh not the righteousness of God. Wherefore lay apart all filthiness and superfluity of naughtiness, and receive with meekness the engrafted word, which is able to save your souls. *James 1:20–21*

In a marriage relationship, how you manage your feelings will determine whether you communicate in a negative or positive way with your spouse. Just because you don't divorce doesn't necessarily mean that your marriage is a success. Is the love within your marriage as strong as it should be? If not, isolate the problems or hindrances within your own life, and make the necessary changes today to improve your marriage. While marital troubles do not have to signal the end of a marriage, without a godly love and commitment, a marriage will never succeed.

If you want to restore the harmony in your relationship but just can't get past some of the emotional barriers or frustrations, try the following: Think about one thing that you adore most about your spouse and recall what it was that drew you to one another in the first place. Then think about how enriched your life has been since you've been together. Now envision having to live the rest of your life without them.

If this exercise does not empower you to drop any contrary thoughts or emotional struggles that are hindering your relationship with your spouse, your faith in Christ needs a serious overhaul.

A Christian marriage is supposed to reflect the harmony between Christ and his undying love for the Church. Marriage is greater than opposing traits of character. When we live in peace and walk in harmony in our marriages we are testifying to the world that the institution of marriage is alive and well.

SECOND MARRIAGES

Before you consider remarriage, make sure you're not still haunted by the ghosts of relationships past. Emotional and spiritual healing from divorce or the death of a spouse takes time. In fact, some studies find that the average person requires three to five years before they can be discerning about a new relationship. They say that experience is the best teacher, but when it comes to relationships this doesn't always hold true. Be careful, because when you're hungry, you'll eat anything. Be honest with yourself and put your lust in check. In a new relationship, feelings tend to develop very quickly.

You need to allow enough time to weed through those emotions and unhook from the past. You need time to unpack your baggage from your last trip. Before you can move forward in a relationship, you must first replace the image in your mind of what a man or a woman is like based on your former relationships.

Many modern marriages, divorces, and even remarriages are contrary to God's plan. Even as sincere Christians, we find ourselves unsure how best to handle these new situations. When there is no clear commandment to guide our behavior, God gives us the Holy Spirit to teach us how to be holy in unholy times.

HOW TO HAVE MARITAL HARMONY

Can two walk together, except they be agreed? *Amos 3:3*

Wouldn't your life be some much better if everyone would just agree with you? Sorry, but this is not going to happen, even in a marriage where both people share a love for God. The prophet Amos was right on target with this one. Just walking in the same direction doesn't mean that you are walking together. Did you know that marriages can end long before divorce? Just because you concede to sleep in the same bed doesn't mean that the marriage is still intact.

Walking together in harmony is what God intended for a true marriage. Not walking with God is like someone singing out of tune. You may get use to hearing it, but you won't enjoy it, neither will anyone else who is forced to listen to it. If you want to have marital harmony, both of you must choose to walk a godly path with the same destination.

> Ointment and perfume rejoice the heart: so doth the sweetness of a man's friend by hearty counsel. *Prov. 27:9*

How many of you men just love it when your wife wears a certain perfume? This verse says that as pleasant as that sense is for you, that's how your wife feels when you really talk to her. Typically, women have a greater need for conversation than men do. It helps her feel united to and bonded with her man. It helps her feel loved and cared for. Husbands need to listen to their wives and honestly assess what they are feeling and thinking. Women process information differently than men and require a more diligent and considerate response.

Not all wives have an appreciation for flowers or a love for chocolate. Why do men keep doing this year after year, occasion after occasion? This type of repeated behavior enforces women's feelings that you just don't get it. Find out what your wife likes or dislikes and find yourself trying to address those needs.

Marriage is designed to address the multiple needs of one another in a holy union under godly counsel. Even though a godly marriage addresses many objectives, the more subtle purpose is to develop and mature two different personalities in a relationship of mutual fellowship and responsibilities. It is a two-way street. To achieve marital harmony is to put your spouse's feelings and interests even before your own. Please understand that this must not be done with a condescending or superficial attitude or a selfish or undermining agenda, but with a genuine attempt to appreciate the love and interests of your spouse. Again, if this is done mutually and sincerely, you will not be just appeasing one another but actually pleasing one another.

> A continual dropping in a very rainy day and a contentious woman are alike. *Prov. 27:15*

This proverb should never be a reflection of a Christian marriage. The analogy of the irritation of the steady drip of water being compared to an argumentative restless spirit is not the makeup of a godly spouse.

When two people love God and truly love one another, the rainfall is more melodious than it is irritating. I love Webster's definition of harmony as an interweaving of different accounts into a single narrative. Doesn't that sound like the mystery of a godly marriage of two people being made one? God made marriage to help us understand more fully His love for the church.

How to Overcome Ghosts of Previous Relationships

Do you believe in ghosts? I'm not talking about those restless souls that go bump in the night, I'm referring to the ghosts of past failed relationships, including all the exes, the children, and extended family members that are thrust into these new, ready-made families. Not silver bullets, not garlic, not even wooden stakes can rid you of these creatures. The only thing that will defeat these types of ghosts are prayers that can reach Calvary's cross.

These "returning spirits" live in very familiar human forms that you know quite well, but if not dealt with properly, they can ruin your life. How do you make sure that the past stays the past, and that your old boyfriends or girlfriends will not return to haunt you?

To rid yourself of these nuisances, the first thing you must do is draw clearly marked boundaries that these ghosts know beyond any doubt that they are never allowed to cross. These boundaries must be respected by your exes and even your children. Needless to say, they will try these newly formed boundaries and if not met with sharp resistance, they will continue to intrude. Ghosts from relationships past remember all of your weaknesses—which is one of the reasons why they keep returning.

Don't you just hate it when in a desperate effort to conceal their own sins, someone says that everyone has skeletons in their closets? Am I the only one that takes offense to that conjecture? Because they choose to live a life of deceit, they conclude that everyone has a dark side. We all walked in darkness at one time in our lives. When we found Christ, we stepped out of the shadows of sin, and turned from the deceit of darkness to the light of Christ. That illumination must be present in your life to rid yourself permanently from these "ghosts" of your past. Remember demons of darkness hate dwelling in the light.

Conventional wisdom teaches that it's not always choosing a better partner but being a better partner. Typically, when choosing a mate the second time around, people look for traits and tendencies exactly opposite from those of their first partner. But if that wisdom is followed, what does that say about your state of mind the first time around? By the way, what does the Holy Spirit say to you concerning your potential mate? The underlining reason contributing to the alarming escalation of divorce among church members is the growing acceptance of the societal view of marriage as a social contract, governed by civil laws, rather than as a sacred covenant instituted by God. Needless to say, in most failed relationships former mates remain bitter and hostile years after their divorce. Children always lose in these situations. Again, remarriage where children are involved should be seriously weighed by what is best for the children and not what is best for you. Remember, if your marriage ends in divorce and children were conceived, their wellbeing takes precedence over your lusts and desires. The hostility of the ex-spouse is often not just restricted to the ex-husband or wife. They may also focus their wrath on your unsuspecting new mate. This is a serious problem in any remarriage. The success or failure of your new marriage heavily depends upon how the new spouse handles their ex-mates—the ghosts of relationships past.

PANDORA'S BOX

In Greek Mythology, Pandora was given a box and instructed by Zeus not to open it. Curiosity got the best of Pandora and of course she opened the box. It is said that when she opened it, she let out all of types of misfortunes and evils upon mankind—greed, envy, vanity, lying, etc. But after all the misfortunes flew out, the last thing that was also contained in the box was hope. Doesn't this mystical tale resemble God's truth about how sin entered into the world? All of what supposedly came out of Pandora's box shared a label of destruction called sin. Whether you are amused by the mythical tale of Zeus and Pandora or convicted by the sin of Adam and Eve, the reality is that sin has become as common as the air we breathe and will never go back from whence it came.

Once the lid has been removed from an unscrupulous marital relationship and the past has been exposed, some very disturbing things are released that become a menace to our society. Consider the summation of the disciples concerning marriage:

And I say unto you, Whosoever shall put away his wife, except it be for fornication, and shall marry another, committeth adultery: and whoso marrieth her which is put away doth commit adultery. His disciples say unto him, If the case of the man be so with his wife, it is not good to marry But he said unto them, All men cannot receive this saying, save they to whom it is given. *Matt. 19:9–11*

If you marry outside of a belief in Christ and then get a divorce, does that count against you? According to the scripture verse above, there are a lot of so-called Christians today in trouble with God. A very sobering fact is that all of these blended families as a result of second, third, and fourth marriages were not ordained of God. Maybe more consideration should be given to the marriage vows before you say 'I do.'

There are obviously unique challenges contained within the secular boundaries of these convenient unions called marriage. As long as a distorted perception of marriage continues to fly under the moral radar undetected, hope of a return to the original blueprint of a godly marriage is quickly disappearing. Of course, we understand and sympathize when a marriage is dissolved due to death, as the apostle Paul shared with the church at Corinth:

The wife is bound by the law as long as her husband liveth; but if her husband be dead, she is at liberty to be married to whom she will; only in the Lord. *1 Cor. 7:39*

The following Old and New Testament passages gives us a glimpse into the mind of God and His intentions for a lifetime commitment to a holy relationship. Listen to the word of God:

And the Pharisees came to him, and asked him, Is it lawful for a man to put away his wife? tempting him.

And he answered and said unto them, What did Moses command you? And they said, Moses suffered to write a bill of divorcement, and to put her away. And Jesus answered and said unto them, For the hardness of your heart he wrote you this precept. But from the beginning of the creation God made them male and female. For this cause shall a man leave his father and mother, and cleave to his wife; And they twain shall be one flesh: so then they are no more twain, but one flesh. What therefore God hath joined together, let not man put asunder. *Mark 10:2–9*

When a man hath taken a wife, and married her, and it come to pass that she find no favour in his eyes, because he hath found some uncleanness in her: then let him write her a bill of divorcement, and give it in her hand, and send her out of his house. And when she is departed out of his house, she may go and be another man's wife. And if the latter husband hate her, and write her a bill of divorcement, and giveth it in her hand, and sendeth her out of his house; or if the latter husband die, which took her to be his wife; Her former husband, which sent her away, may not take her again to be his wife, after that she is defiled; for that is abomination before the Lord: and thou shalt not cause the land to sin, which the Lord thy God giveth thee for an inheritance. *Deut. 24:1–4*

Many of the modern marriages, divorces, and even remarriages are contrary to God's plan. Even as sincere Christians, we find ourselves without a documented playbook regarding these unions, and just winging it as we go along. Thank God for the Holy Spirit that improvises when there is no clear commandment. The Holy Spirit teaches us how to be holy in unholy times when God's commandments are silent. We won't dare say it out loud, but when we do things contrary to the Spirit, we're praying, "Lord please bless this mess!"

How do we move forward on a godly track when a marriage has ended and children are involved? Dating as practiced today by many so-called Christians is ungodly. Christian dating is important but true stepfamily relationships start with the wedding. Children are sometimes tolerant, even encouraging of their parent's new romance, but they frequently change their tune when real stepfamily life begins.

Could you imagine the confusion involved if your new husband has to referee between his current and former wife? In that situation, should the husband always defend his current wife, or get into the same corner at times with the mother of his children? The new husband or wife can easily sabotage their marriage by unskillfully handling these situations.

Additional consideration must be given to the in-laws that are still sulking about the ex-spouse's departure from the family. It's too bad that divorces don't come with a checklist before being granted. Will you be able to attend church, school functions, extended family holidays, and community social events with your new mate's ex-spouse? How can the new spouse avoid feeling like she is walking in the footsteps of the woman who came before her? It seems that no one ever warns the new wife, the woman who marries a divorced man, that an ambush may await her.

Anyone marrying a divorcee should heed the warning signs. If your potential mate cannot handle his or her ex-spouse before you're married, what makes you think that there will be any difference afterwards? Don't fool yourself, the same woman or man who is the mother or father of your stepchildren will continue to make their presence known in your new home.

The first wife may continue to be a part of your life throughout your remarriage, especially if children resulted from this union.

And here's another sobering fact, this doesn't necessarily change when these children become adults! Graduations, weddings, the birth of shared grandchildren and their subsequent special occasions, all these will mandate get-togethers of the "original" family. Still want to remarry?

You may want to rethink your remarriage fantasies and consider the realities of stepfamily life. You first must understand the challenges of a blended family and then make an informed choice about remarriage. Again, you must seriously consider the fact that remarriage may prove advantageous for adults but a loss for the children. In many instances, in the back of the children's mind, what they really want is for mom and dad to reunite, so for them the new marriage is a loss. Given this fact, if you still decide to remarry, you should discuss a strategy for your parenting roles especially when the children are still young.

Should the biological parent be the main source of discipline in the home? Sorry, but this is not covered in the playbook. Consideration must be given to the mental and emotional maturity of the parents and the stability of the children. Getting the children to call the perceived intruder to their family as father or mother is not the battle to be fought. The question that you should ask yourself when going into a new marriage is this, "can I play second fiddle to his or her children?" Biological parents can't just switch their loyalties—it feels like they're betraying their children. This is a broad cloak to hide behind for a sorry parent, because they may lean on this as an excuse for lack of structure or discipline. Despite these struggles, the new couple must learn to nurture their relationship and not place the children in the middle of conflict. Keep in mind that this blended family structure was not ordained by God. Getting new marriages to work in a godly fashion will require complete spiritual submission and guidance of the Holy Spirit. As Christians, we are to create ghost-proof homes that can house godly efforts to rebuild what a secular society has destroyed.

"I hear you knocking but you can't come in" should be your new theme song! Not dealing spiritually with the mistakes or ghosts of your past will ruin any chances that you may have to secure a happy future.

PASTOR ROBINSON'S SUNDAY SCHOOL LESSON
BUILDING MARITAL INTIMACY

Many marriages are running on human love, and this is the reason why they are failing to bring the fulfillment and satisfaction they are designed to bring. How can you determine the difference between human and divine love?

Gen. 2:18

18 And the Lord God said, It is not good that the man should be alone.

The above scripture reference speaks to the need of an intimate companionship with our mate. Our intimate relationship with God is designed to be shared with others, especially our mates. When Adam and Eve severed their intimate relationship with God, their marriage relationship suffered and the finger pointing started.

As human beings, we all have the same spiritual, emotional, and physical needs as Adam. We are all born into the world needing attention, affection, approval, and comfort. Marriage was created by God to fill these needs through an intimate relationship with our mates. Unfortunately, when we speak of intimacy in marriage, we think mostly of the physical relationship. True intimacy in marriage begins with the spiritual rather than the physical.

Matt. 16:25

25 For whosoever will save his life shall lose it: and whosoever will lose his life for my sake shall find it.

Many Christians never discover intimacy in marriage because they are afraid that they will lose their personal identity. Do you still feel reluctant to show affection to your spouse in front of your old friends and family? Wives, do you feel belittled or ashamed to serve your husband at a banquet function when he could just as easily serve himself? If so, you may still be trying to save your positive self-image of a proud, independent woman—in the meantime your marriage could be eroding.

1 John 4:11

11 Beloved, if God so loved us, we ought also to love one another.

Col. 3:19

19 Husbands, love your wives, and be not bitter against them.

Intimacy in a marriage will grow when you are able to adjust (not lower) your expectations toward one another. We have to face the reality that husbands and wives are often at different spiritual and intellectual maturity levels. If either of you are condescending, you will never understand companionship and intimacy.

Matt. 6:33

33 But seek ye first the kingdom of God, and his righteousness; and all these things shall be added unto you.

When you mutually work together to fulfill the purpose of God, the Holy Spirit will draw you together in the process.

Prov. 17:14

14 The beginning of strife is as when one letteth out water: therefore leave off contention, before it be meddled with.

Often couples enter into a destructive habit of arguing and picking on one another. It seems that no matter what one says, the other finds fault with it. Does this mean that these couples have stopped loving one another? Not necessarily. It could mean that they cannot communicate together spiritually. They cannot share the intimate details of their lives and that is why they continuously argue. In order to overcome this lack of intimacy, godly couples need to consciously learn to communicate with each another in the Spirit of Christ.

James 1:21–22

21 Wherefore lay apart all filthiness and superfluity of naughtiness, and receive with meekness the engrafted word, which is able to save your souls.

22 But be ye doers of the word, and not hearers only, deceiving your own selves.

Do you honestly want an intimate spiritual marital relationship? How much time do you invest in open discussion to accomplish this? Remember, the deeper the relationship the more time and effort necessary. You are fooling yourself to think that a good marriage naturally evolves out of a beautiful marriage ceremony. Believe it or not, the marriage starts after the ceremony.

My Testimony of Marital Harmony

First Lady Patricia M. Robinson

My husband, Pastor Salem Robinson, Jr., and I were married on a pleasant evening on August 19, 1976. I'll never forget the day of our wedding. The sun was just setting and our family and friends were hustling around in preparation. My future husband's parents held our wedding in their home. The ceremony took place in their backyard and it was filled with blue and yellow streamers. We chose to put the emphasis on the marriage over the expense of an elaborate wedding.

I was guided down the stairs, surrounded by those who set the stage for this wonderful occasion. When I turned the corner, I searched through the crowd to find Salem's face at the end of the aisle. We made our vows before God and in the company of our family and friends and became husband and wife.

About two weeks before, we had both made another important vow when we accepted Jesus Christ as our personal Savior. Shortly afterwards, my husband asked me to be his wife and companion in Christ.

At my husband's request and to avoid any temptation, we agreed not to be in each other's company for the brief two-week period that we were engaged before the marriage ceremony. Salem sent me several beautiful letters and we talked on the phone, but we didn't visit each other. We didn't know it then, but God had plans to use us as an example of proper Christian dating habits and to call Salem into the ministry.

I know that if Salem had asked me to marry him before we both accepted Christ, I would have reacted differently: more along the line of "What? I don't think so!" I knew that there was no trust or commitment to our relationship then because of the path we were both traveling on.

There was no doubt in my mind about whether or not I loved Salem or that he loved me, but at that time, we weren't walking together in the fear and love of God as spoken of in the Bible. We would have united in unholy matrimony and had a relationship based on lust and without harmony. Our marriage as sinners could not stand on just our love alone and would have ended up the same as any other worldly marriage, a disaster.

Marital harmony can only exist when both of you follow the plan that is set forth in the Bible. When we shed the ideals of feminism, then we can accept the biblical order that the man is the head of the home. Sarah is noted in the Bible as one who had no problem with reverencing her husband. Every Christian wife should follow Sarah's example.

Harmony is inevitable when there is mutual respect. As a Christian woman, I don't view being under subjection to my husband as a sign of weakness. Unfortunately, many women today see it as demeaning to surrender their will to the pattern set by God. This type of thinking will make it impossible to achieve harmony in a marriage.

The harmony that exists in our home is due to our desire to follow God. I must admit that it is easy to walk in harmony in a marriage when your husband is totally dedicated to serving God. You see, a godly woman will not have a problem following a godly man.

I feel blessed by God to have the opportunity to experience this beautiful godly marriage.

A Blended Family in Christ

Deaconess Lutrecia Oshoko

The average home today is made up of blended families. I was divorced with two little girls, ages 2 and 6, when I met my husband, David Oshoko. By the grace of God, he fell into the mix of our ready-made family. I came to our relationship and our new marriage with lots of baggage—emotional baggage, financial baggage, and my most precious baggage, my two daughters.

My new husband had his work cut out for him, but I thank God that his love for God and his love for me and for my children provided him with the willingness to take on this big task. The responsibility of making this marriage work and keeping it solid fell mainly upon my husband. He was the one with the most understanding and patience. God has given him plenty of the fruits of the Spirit.

Through the grace of God, he's able to be the provider and the image of a Christian father to all of our children, and to make up for the shortcomings of the girls' biological father. My husband was able to gain the respect of my family and the trust and love of my mother because of the life that he's led before them. He's also learned how to prayerfully interact with my ex-husband and his extended family.

My husband's abilities as a Christian husband and father soar far above what I could have ever dreamed or hoped for. Not only is he a great father to all of our children, he is a hard worker and provider for his family.

He adores and spoils me but the best thing about him is that he is a man that loves God. What more could a Christian woman ask for? God has sent me the mate that was meant for me.

Did I know when we started our relationship that my husband was my soul mate and someone God had made up that was perfect for me? No! This is often the case when you depend on your own ideas about finding a mate, rather than depending on God's will. When you depend on your own ideas, you enter a relationship for variety of reasons, and many times not the right ones.

A relationship that has not been built on the foundation of God makes for one that's vulnerable when the storms of life come. We've been through many storms as a blended family. At one time, the cares and the burdens of life pulled at me. I was making everything my priority except my husband and my children. When you are child of God, there's only so far that He will allow you to go before He snatches you back into his arms—and snatch me back is exactly what He did! Little did I know that my life would drastically change for the better after my husband, who is from Nigeria, had to return home for emergency medical care after a visit to Africa.

While in Africa, David suffered a seizure that caused him to fall. He broke his shoulder and while being treated, we learned that the seizure was caused by a brain tumor that needed to be removed immediately.

When I was faced with his sickness, I was snapped back into reality. I had to pray for strength and find out what was really important to me and what my priorities should be in life. This would be the beginning of my search and discovery of what true love really is.

I was raised in the church and taught that there is no love apart from God. When you try to live your life apart from God, you leave your life to luck or as we call it, a sinner's faith. Before I came to truly know Christ, I tried to live my life apart from Him, but everything that happened to me was by no means lucky.

God has always had a will and plan for me, even when I didn't understand what that plan was and didn't want to accept His will. I needed help to rediscover and sort out what God's plan was and still is in my life. I'm blessed that I knew just the people to help me.

When I was growing up, I had godparents who became my dad and my second mom. Out of everyone I've ever known, they exemplified a couple who loves each other, and who love and fear God. They always had a love for the truth (that in my younger years I thought was extreme).

My godparents—who are now also my pastor and first lady—helped me to develop a new relationship, not only with God, but with my husband and with my children.

Relationships take time and developing my own personal relationship with God, my husband, and my children has had its challenges. Something new is always exciting and fearful and tests a person's thought process, especially when you have preconceived notions of how something should or should not be.

My new relationship with God challenges me to totally surrender my will and my ways to the will of God. My new relationship in Christ with my husband has grown into a deep love and friendship. My commitment to him is until death do us part. The new relationship with my children demands that I mold myself into being a Christian mother first and not their friend.

These new relationships have by no means been easy and Satan is always there to discourage us. Through my own stubbornness, I've made many terrible choices, but I know that everything I've gone through has made me a better person.

Every day is a new day for me to work on cultivating these relationships so that I can experience the joy and happiness that God has set forth in this life. I'm striving each day to obtain eternal life filled with ultimate joy.

A Christian Marriage

Bro. Michael Medearis

I never thought that such a deep and abiding love for my wife, Angela, would require me to love God first. It scares me when I consider what might have happened had I gotten married before I became a Christian or before my wife also accepted Jesus into her life.

We dated as sinners for a short time, and we probably appeared to be a promising young couple. I was a sophomore in college with aspirations toward journalism and politics. She was a freshman at a school nearby who had already shown a talent for writing. We both came from church-going, middle class families.

Most people didn't see that I had a dark and ugly side that I kept hidden to most people. I was sexually active at an early age, was on my way to being an alcoholic, and was quick to defend my recreational use of marijuana. In addition, I was also addicted to pornography. Angela was not aware of most of my issues because like so many others, I put on a good front.

Eventually, she would have found out about the "real" me, but I was blessed that God loved me enough to give me the opportunity to change my life by accepting Jesus' sacrifice on the cross. As it turned out, Angela had her own issues that I was not aware of since she was a virgin and did not use alcohol or any type of drugs. On the surface, she was a morally good person, but was hiding the fact that what she did not do outwardly had already taken place in her imagination and conscience. She did not really know or understand the true meaning of Christianity either.

The very essence of our love for each other is rooted in the reality of God having loved us first. We both know and understand why God sent His Son, Jesus Christ, into the world—it was to show us what real love is.

God gave me a perfect opportunity to start all over again with my perfect soul mate. So many people who marry young often have short lived and disastrous relationships. For us however, the fact that we were so young and clueless turned out to be a blessing. I have been blessed with the opportunity to grow up with a beautiful woman who was also growing up. After over 33 years of marriage, we are still growing in the Lord together.

I never know exactly what my wife is going to do next. Just when I think that I do, she throws me a curve. The fact that she changes her mind so often used to be somewhat exasperating to my analytical, pragmatic side, but this has actually helped me as a Christian. I realize that to be open to God means that you are willing to change your way of thinking and doing things before He can bless you. My wife brings out the playful side of me. I love being a husband to this woman. I couldn't see myself as happy with anyone else.

Today's relationships seem to be as disposable as chewing gum when the flavor is gone. My son, Lorenzo, once asked me if I was still physically attracted to my wife after all these years. I explained to him that I was, but that the reasons went far beyond just my physical attraction to her. I tell people that one of the reasons our marriage has lasted so long is that unlike many couples today, we did not live together before we got married. I thank God for blessing us with a continuing sense of excitement about each other as we grow closer together. In our relationship, we not only consider the effects of our actions toward each other, but more importantly, how our actions appear before God.

This mutual understanding is reinforced by the biblical teachings and godly counsel of our beloved pastor, Salem Robinson, Jr. If we need marriage counseling, we seek it out. It isn't always possible for a couple to resolve a problem in a marriage themselves. If my wife and I can't resolve a marital problem, we go to our pastor for prayer and guidance. Through his teachings, I have found that there is no problem or issue in our marriage that cannot be solved by applying God's word along with the guidance of His Holy Spirit.

Real love requires the personal sacrifice of your wants, the surrender of your will, and a complete trust and a total commitment that transcends any human circumstance. This is the perfect love that Jesus Christ showed when He lived on earth. It was only after I accepted Jesus Christ that I learned how to express this true love, which is God's love, to my wife. We both had to learn how to express that love to others. I realize that this may be hard to understand in a world where selfishness and self-preservation is the rule. The scriptures provide us with insight into this biblical concept:

> Greater love hath no man than this, that a man lay down his life for his friends. *2 John 15:13*

This is not merely a religious platitude. My wife is truly my best friend. As Christ died for me on the cross, I have to be willing to die—that is, give up my old ways of living a sinful life—in order to have the peace, joy, and contentment that God has brought to me, my wife, and my family.

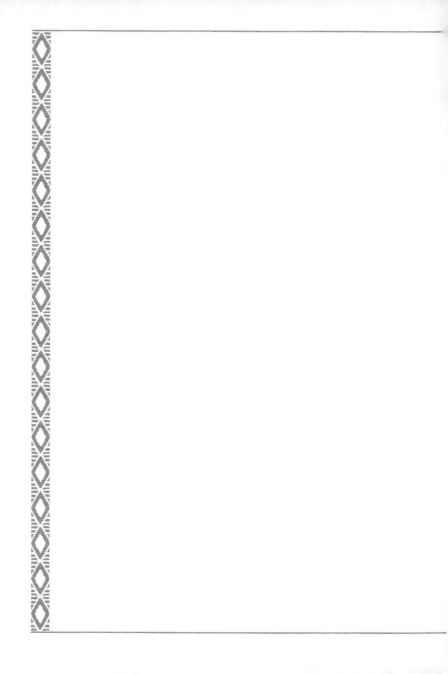

Chapter Nine: Godly Children
ANGELA'S TESTIMONY

I love children and I've enjoyed being a mother and a grandmother. My husband and I have one biological daughter, Deanna, who is now a young adult with a daughter of her own named Anysa. We also have a son, Lorenzo, who we've mentored since he was nine years old and in a special foster care program. Lorenzo "adopted us" last year when he was seventeen.

My parenting skills with each child have been different, because my growth as a Christian has been at different levels as my children have grown and matured into young adulthood. I was 20 years old when I had Deanna and to say that I was unprepared for motherhood would be an understatement! By the grace of God, my husband and I worked together to try to fulfill the little that we knew about how to raise a godly child. I cringe now at some of the mistakes we made as young parents, but thank the Lord for His mercy on our ignorance!

We raised our daughter in the church and did our best to instill a love for God in her by example. As children often do, she strayed away from the things we taught her when she got out on her own. I know from my experience with my own child that the word of God is true: "Train up a child in the way he should go: and when he is old, he will not depart from it," (Prov. 22:6).

Deanna accepted Christ as her personal savior on January 12, 2007 the same day that I had accepted Christ 32 years ago! That was a wonderful day, and it is a blessing that we now share the same spiritual birthday. Deanna is beautiful inside and out, extremely talented, and smart; however, her decision to accept Christ is the accomplishment that we're the most proud of.

Our relationship has totally changed now that Deanna is a Christian. While I'll always be her mother, and I'll always try to help and advise her in anyway that I can, she is also my Sister in Christ, and a great help to me as well. I love the patience she has and her loving spirit. Even though Deanna is an adult, her co-workers often compliment us on how well we've raised her. We refuse to take any credit for the wonderful young woman she's grown to become by the grace of God. Even though my husband and I were young parents, and there were many things we didn't know about raising a child, our decision to instill a love for God in our daughter has had a lasting impact on her life, and on our grandchild's life. We both greatly admire our daughter and her new commitment to raise her child by being a good example as a single, Christian mother.

The decisions you make about how you want to live your life and the way that you decide to raise your child will have repercussions for generations to come. Our decision to accept Christ and to raise our daughter to love God changed our child's life. My daughter's decision to accept Christ has had a positive impact on my granddaughter, Anysa. Anysa made a decision to accept Christ and to set an example as a Christian in high school. It is possible to raise a godly child in an ungodly world if you submit yourself to Christ and let Him show you how to be a parent.

Just when my husband and I breathed a sigh of relief about our daughter and granddaughter, we became parents again! Never in our wildest dreams did we ever think that we'd be raising a child in our fifties! But that's what the Lord had planned for our lives, and we've accepted it.

Because our son was abandoned by his parents in infancy, passed from one foster home to the next, and had been rejected again and again, we've had to prayerfully overcome many things.

Since Lorenzo didn't become a part of our family until he was seventeen, it has been a struggle to help him learn all of the things he needs to know in order to make the right choices about his spiritual life and his future.

We have to patiently teach Lorenzo simple things that other children are taught from birth. The way we live seems strange to him because he's never had a mother or a father or been part of a family, especially a Christian family. I can't seem to cook enough food or to hug Lorenzo enough to fill up all the empty places he has inside, but I'm trying. My husband patiently tries to teach him the things he needs to know to become a decent young man. We've got a lot of work to do with Lorenzo, but we know that by the grace of God, we'll have the strength to do it.

We pray for Lorenzo every day because we know that we only have a short time to prepare him for life as an adult in a hard, cold world. We also know that God has placed Lorenzo in our home so that he can see a daily example of a family that loves the Lord, and so that he could be loved for himself for the first time.

I've learned many things from my children and gained a wealth of spiritual gifts I wouldn't have obtained without the benefit of motherhood. Prayer changes things and it is one of the most powerful tools in a parent's spiritual arsenal. I've learned to pray for and about my children. I've learned to be patient even when I've said something for the hundredth time. I've learned that the love of God can be shown by preparing a child's favorite meal, spending time doing the things that they love, and most of all, by setting a constant, steadfast example of a Christian before them.

In an uncertain and insecure world, our children need parents who are rooted in Christ. While the best of all possible situations would be that every child who is born into this world be blessed with two parents who love the Lord, each other, and their child, this is seldom the case. No matter what your situation as a Christian parent may be, you have the blessing of knowing that you can turn to the Lord in prayer about every situation and receive the strength that you need to be the best parent you can be through the grace of God.

COMMENTS BY PASTOR SALEM ROBINSON, JR.

Parenting is one of the most important skills to have, especially in today's fast-paced, high-tech world. Some parents rear their children to become moral, productive, and responsible adults, while other parents rear their children to become immoral, unproductive, and irresponsible. In fact, these parents are just being lazy and are not really trusting God themselves. You must ask yourself: Up to now, have you raised wise children? Are you really parenting your children for success or setting them up for failure?

> And that from a child thou hast known the holy scriptures, which are able to make thee wise unto salvation through faith which is in Christ Jesus. *2 Tim. 3:15*

> Josiah was eight years old when he began to reign, and he reigned in Jerusalem one and thirty years. And he did that which was right in the sight of the Lord, and walked in the ways of David his father, and declined neither to the right hand, nor to the left. *2 Chron. 34:1–2*

Every child is different. Some children are extroverted, while others are introverted. Some children are athletic, while others are academic. Some of a child's personality is genetic, but not all. This is not an excuse to neglect your responsibility to your child. Yes, genes do have some affect on a child's behavior; but their environment and the way a child is parented, also have a great influence as well.

As parents, our life experiences are a valuable resource that, if used prayerfully, will benefit both the parent and the child. The unwillingness to share our past failures in life with our children will deprive them of a valuable source of information. Our experiences, our knowledge, and our past failures should all be shared with our children so that they will not repeat them. Let them know that the Christian person that you are today has been shaped by the powers of God through faith. As a Christian parent, you will become a source of knowledge and consolation to your children as they encounter their own struggles.

My sons, Timothy and Trey, both made a profession of faith early in their lives. By the grace of God, my wife and I lived a Christian life before them. As Christian parents, our emphasis was on living our faith before them rather than forcing them to measure up to some religious standard.

Early in our marriage we made a vow to God and to one another to set an example of how a man and woman in Christ should love one another. After more than thirty years of marriage, I still thank the Lord for giving me this life to share with my wife. When our children were little, the first thing I would do upon entering our home after a days work was embrace and kiss my wife. I intentionally wanted our boys to see what they called "mushy stuff," because I wanted them to witness how a man is supposed to love his wife.

As a man before God, I not only wanted my wife to adore me but I also wanted my sons to respect my integrity in Christ. I wouldn't do anything that would compromise my commitment to them or to God. Even today, I thank God that they still come to me for advice, knowing that my love for them and my fear of God will have me speak from the heart of truth.

Fatherhood hasn't changed. Motherhood hasn't changed, and the anatomy of a woman still manifests the truth of God's design and purpose. The void in the home today is because of the absent parents. Our children are left to raise themselves while we run for cover from our own guilt and hide behind rationalizations and excuses. As a parent, we often give our children everything but what they really need—and that is ourselves.

Revealing Your Past to Protect Your Children's Future

I was asked by a young father for any advice or points of wisdom I could give him about raising boys. He asked me if there was anything he could do to discourage their involvement in drugs and if it was inevitable that their teenage years would be filled with rebellion.

I told him that you raise godly children by leveraging your life experiences, both good and bad, as a resource of knowledge to aid in their social development. Let them know that you were not born old and boring and that you understand their struggles and fears because you too went down the same trails and veered from the main paths.

I advised him not to follow the previous generation's sworn secrecy of silence about their sins and failures. Exposure of your past will not cause you to be diminished in the eyes of your children, but rather, it will elevate you as a living testimony of God's power to change.

In raising children, you must be consistent in judgment. Always affirm your love for them so that it is never in question. Always do what is best for them, regardless of their approval. Don't just tell them that character matters, show them. Be impeccable in your character and their respect for you will help them be subordinate to the authority of God and rebellion will not be a part of their formative years.

This is not only a successful formula for raising boys but also is effective for raising girls. It is imperative for parents to understand that rebellion in your children may be more directed to your obviously flawed hypocrisies than external challenges or a need for conformity outside the home. Not all teens will be disrespectful and rebel against their parents.

Invisible Parents

When you hear about children caught up in the devastating world of cyber porn or building bombs in their bedrooms, you have to ask yourself, where were their parents? These invisible parents with their pretense of a hands-off parenting style are really only attempting to disguise their laziness and emotional immaturity. Just as Adam stood by and did nothing while the serpent beguiled his wife, Eve, in the Garden of Eden, so often is the case with these uncommitted parents.

Children are very smart and usually know their parents much better than their parents understand them. Many times, parents are unaware that their children are using manipulation to get their own way. As children mature, many parents are surprised or shocked that their child could behave in a way that brings a reproach upon them, even going so far as to commit serious criminal offenses.

> The rod and reproof give wisdom: but a child left to himself brings his mother to shame. *Prov. 29:15*

Some children act in deviant ways and that behavior goes unpunished at home. When parents are not present not only is there no role model for the child, but no one to correct bad behavior. Many parents take for granted that their children will turn out just fine because they have provided good food, good clothes, a good house, good toys, etc. To them, that is all that's required to be a good parent.

I realize there may be some theological rebuttals to my next statement, but I will still wade in the waters of truth by saying that there is nothing in this world that we can take with us when we die. However, by investing time and energy into your children's spiritual wellbeing, you can take them with you to heaven.

> If thy children will keep my covenant and my testimony that I shall teach them, their children shall also sit upon thy throne for evermore. *Ps. 132:12*

You can choose to neglect your responsibilities to train your children in the ways of God, but in the last days, upon receiving their sentence of eternal destruction, both you and your children will suffer for your neglect.

There are some creatures that we can look to for wisdom like the ant:

> Go to the ant, thou sluggard; consider her ways, and be wise: Which having no guide, overseer, or ruler, Provideth her meat in the summer, [and] gathereth her food in the harvest. *Prov. 6:6–8*

God is telling us humans that we can learn from even His smallest creation, the ant, but when it comes to parenting wisdom, don't follow after the ostrich!

> Gavest thou the goodly wings unto the peacocks? or wings and feathers unto the ostrich? Which leaveth her eggs in the earth, and warmeth them in dust, And forgetteth that the foot may crush them, or that the wild beast may break them. She is hardened against her young ones, as though [they were] not hers: her labour is in vain without fear; Because God hath deprived her of wisdom, neither hath he imparted to her understanding. *Job 39:13–17*

I know parents who seem to be a direct descendant of the ostrich when it comes to handling their young! There is no visible sign of compassionate love, they give no guidance to their children and do nothing to protect them, and somehow they have the audacity to want some credit for their child's survival! A tree is known by the fruit it bears, so you cannot be ungodly and raise godly children. Likewise, you cannot be godly yourself and be an invisible parent. You can only attribute so much to ignorance, after that is weighed in the balance, what remains are the choices you made.

Guidance, Supervision, and Discipline

Even in a secular society, we understand that reward and punishment are the two forces that influence human behavior. Think about it, most people go to work and perform their job adequately, because they get paid (reward). Most people don't skip work or perform their job poorly, because they fear getting fired (punishment).

News flash! Children need supervision. The more you supervise your child, the more of a chance your child will become a moral, productive, and responsible adult. The less you supervise your child, the less chance your child will have to be successful emotionally and spiritually. When parenting children, you get what you put into it. A child's brain isn't fully developed, and if they do not fear God, they will struggle with sound judgment and insight. That's why children require the supervision of responsible adults to ensure they are making godly decisions in their lives.

Children in crime-ridden ghettos can claim an excuse for bad behavior because their parents are probably nowhere to be found or are too busy getting high on drugs or sleeping around. So it's not surprising that many of these children grow up to be huge disappointments, committing crime and going to prison. But what is truly sad is when parents from relatively economically stable homes, are too lazy to even supervise their child or to assist them in developing normally.

It is emotionally healthy for our children to try to exercise their independence and define their own identities, but at the same time, our children want and need guiding principles from their parents to help them. Our teens need their parent's guidance about how to make sound choices while spreading their wings.

> The rod and reproof give wisdom: but a child left to himself bringeth his mother to shame. *Prov. 29:15*

For several centuries, the phrase "spare the rod and spoil the child" was the rule of thumb for disciplining children. Do I agree with this phrase? Yes, if the phrase is interpreted figuratively rather than just literally. The rod is not always a wooden rod, but punishment in general.

THE PARENTAL CHRISTIAN ROLE MODEL

Parents can model positive behaviors by being truthful with their children when they are young and telling them they can expect the same honesty in return. If they catch you in a lie, they justify that it is okay to play the same game. Our children are never too young to understand the concept of being honest.

As parents, you must exhibit honesty at all times. If you demonstrate to them that lying to the telemarketer or stretching the truth with your friends to ease your own discomfort is okay, your children will do the same.

Whether we like it or not, our children are a reflection of who we are. Setting a good example is critical to establishing reasonable boundaries for your teens. If you show little regard for the rules you establish for your teens, they will place little value on them, too.

A consciousness of God should be encouraged at an early age to combat this growing age of perversion and promiscuity. It takes more than just information about sex to corral the unrestrained lusts that are preying upon our children. Real faith in God and Christ is the only effectively proven antidote for the sick perversions of sin.

A CHILD'S FAITH AND THE PLAN OF SALVATION

Some parents question whether young children can genuinely be saved because they feel that children are too immature to understand the complex theological issues involved. These parents don't understand the simplicity of salvation or that it has nothing to do with theology.

While Christian parents may have some initial concerns about their child confusing enthusiasm for genuine conviction and commitment, they know that salvation is real. Again, as godly parents, you must show your children that Christ is the center of your life by aligning your personal priorities with your profession of faith. If Christ is not your true priority, neither will He be sacred to your children.

Some parents feel a child has to reach a certain age before he can make any spiritual decisions. This is often called the "age of accountability" because of this biblical reference about Jesus:

> And the child grew, and waxed strong in spirit, filled with wisdom: and the grace of God was upon him. Now his parents went to Jerusalem every year at the feast of the Passover. And when he was twelve years old, they went up to Jerusalem after the custom of the feast. *Luke 2:40–42*

One would be more consistent with scripture to realize that at whatever age a child is capable of learning simple biblical truths, that is the age he or she becomes accountable to God for acting on those truths. Again, raising godly children is not about making religious proselytes.

> And they brought young children to him, that he should touch them: and [his] disciples rebuked those that brought [them]. But when Jesus saw [it], he was much displeased, and said unto them, Suffer the little children to come unto me, and forbid them not: for of such is the kingdom of God. Verily I say unto you, Whosoever shall not receive the kingdom of God as a little child, he shall not enter therein. *Mark 10:13–15*

Christian adults are told through the word of God to emulate the implicit, pure, uncritical trust which children exemplify. Some of the children who were brought to Christ were no doubt too young to understand the significance of this holy encounter, but they could at least feel the tenderness of His love.

> And that from a child thou hast known the holy scriptures, which are able to make thee wise unto salvation through faith which is in Christ Jesus. *2 Tim. 3:15*

In this verse, the apostle Paul is reminding Timothy of the impact that the word of God and a God-fearing mother had upon his life as a child. Timothy's mother was wise to instruct and instill the values of God into her child. God has given numerous biblical instructions to parents to take personal responsibility for their children's spiritual education. Christian parents will not be held guiltless for their negligence.

As Christian parents, once we come into the knowledge that raising godly children is our duty to perform, that knowledge, if not acted upon, becomes sin and is punishable by God.

PASTOR ROBINSON'S SUNDAY SCHOOL LESSON

HOW NOT TO BE A DYSFUNCTIONAL FAMILY

After surrendering your life to Christ, your family is your first and most influential bond. Families can be wonderful when their members love, respect, and support each other. This can only be accomplished by standing in the power of faith in God.

Ps. 51:5

5 Behold, I was shapen in iniquity; and in sin did my mother conceive me.

Ps. 58:3

3 The wicked are estranged from the womb: they go astray as soon as they be born, speaking lies.

Belief in the above passages is paramount to godly parenting. Our natural birth has instilled a sinful nature that is passed on to every child born of a woman. God has ordained the family to provide the insight and godly instructions to bring that child back into the fellowship with him.

1 Sam. 1:11

11 And she vowed a vow, and said, O Lord of hosts, if thou wilt indeed look on the affliction of thine handmaid, and remember me, and not forget thine handmaid, but wilt give unto thine handmaid a man child, then I will give him unto the Lord all the days of his life, and there shall no razor come upon his head.

Consider this: try to list some godly traits that you admire in your children, that were developed first in your life. These traits should be ones that were instrumental in planting and nurturing your child.

Deut. 4:9

9 Only take heed to thyself, and keep thy soul diligently, lest thou forget the things which thine eyes have seen, and lest they depart from thy heart all the days of thy life: but teach them thy sons, and thy sons' sons.

Deut. 6:6–9

6 And these words, which I command thee this day, shall be in thine heart:

7 And thou shalt teach them diligently unto thy children, and shalt talk of them when thou sittest in thine house, and when thou walkest by the way, and when thou liest down, and when thou risest up.

8 And thou shalt bind them for a sign upon thine hand, and they shall be as frontlets between thine eyes.

9 And thou shalt write them upon the posts of thy house, and on thy gates.

Children learn who they are as emotional beings from the role modeling of their parents. You've heard the old saying, "Monkey see, monkey do." The saying, "Do as I say, not as I do," does not work with children. Spiritually dishonest parents cannot be emotionally healthy adult role models for their children.

In order for the family to function as intended by God, the home must be an example of love and respect. When husband and wife love each other as Christ loved the church, they are then qualified to be parents. Only with this type of love will the home become a stable, healthy environment for children. Your job is to win your children to God.

Chasten means to train a child and is used throughout the New Testament of believers, not unbelievers. For example, the same word for chasten is used in Hebrews 12:5–6: "And you have forgotten the exhortation which speaks to you as to sons: 'My son, do not despise the chastening of the Lord, nor be discouraged when you are rebuked by Him; for whom the Lord loves He chastens, and scourges every son whom He receives.'"

Children need to know the ethics you practice are found in God's principles for living. No one will ever have a greater influence on your children than you. That is why you are commanded to lead your family spiritually.

Prov. 22:6

6 Train up a child in the way he should go: and when he is old, he will not depart from it.

We need to conform to a biblical view of the family. To have a biblical view of our families we must understand the priorities of husband, wife, and children. God must be first!

Luke 14:26–27

26 If any man come to me, and hate not his father, and mother, and wife, and children, and brethren, and sisters, yea, and his own life also, he cannot be my disciple.

27 And whosoever doth not bear his cross, and come after me, cannot be my disciple.

2 Tim. 3:16

16 All scripture is given by inspiration of God, and is profitable for doctrine, for reproof, for correction, for instruction in right-eousness.

In order to live fully as a happy, healthy Christian parent, you must instill Christian values in your children, and provide them with a living example of a godly life.

RAISING GODLY CHILDREN

FIRST LADY PATRICIA M. ROBINSON

 I love the story of how Hannah prayed for a male child for the sole purpose of giving him back to the Lord:

> And she vowed a vow, and said, O Lord of hosts, if thou wilt indeed look on the affliction of thine handmaid, and remember me, and not forget thine handmaid, but wilt give unto thine handmaid a man child, then I will give him unto the Lord all the days of his life, and there shall no razor come upon his head. *1 Sam. 1:11*

I too made vows asking God to give me the ability to raise my children in the fear and admonition of the Lord. Most parents in America have the opportunity to raise a child to be strong and healthy. Raising godly children is often confused with raising a child to be religious. Taking them to church will not always result in godly behavior. Godly behavior in our children starts with godly behavior in the parents.

I'm blessed of God to be married to a godly man who esteems God's presence in our home. Needless to say, this makes my job as a mother a whole lot easier. Let me tell you a little secret, embracing Christianity was the best choice of my life. I love the Christian life that I live. Now that I have something that is real and profitable for me, I try to instill those godly values in my children. Children are wise enough to test how real we are in our faith and they will try us before they can be convinced that Christianity is real and a good choice for them.

It is our job as parents to provide the best Christian environment for our children. My husband and I realized that this was an opportunity to afford our children the same confidence and freedom of choice that we had by filling our home with the right spirit to help them develop into what we consider to be productive citizens.

As parents, we made a vow between us that we would present a life in Christ before them that would give our children fond memories for years to come. As a mother, I loved them but I never lost sight of my duty to train them. The famous quote "It takes a village to raise a child" seems to leave an excuse for some parents not to own up to their responsibilities. Sure, we all should welcome help from other loving and caring family and friends. But you have to make sure that they share the same Christian value system that is dear to you.

While I feel strongly that discipline is to be practiced when raising children, others may feel that it's cruel and unnecessary. Godly discipline, in my point of view, is merely a way to set the boundaries for your children, while teaching them what is good and safe for them and what is not acceptable.

As a mother, I was mindful to be consistent in teaching godly values to my children. It is easy to teach them to be appreciative and to say "please" and "thank you," but you have to remind them again and again to be polite and courteous. Remember, they are in training throughout the different stages of their lives, and this is just the beginning. That means you must be there for them, first setting the example in your own life and holding firm to the godly principles you've instilled in them. You have to remind them over and over again until they understand what is expected of them and it becomes natural.

> To every thing there is a season, and a time to every purpose under the heaven. *Eccles. 3:1*

I often find myself tapping into some of Solomon's wisdom when raising my children. There is a proper time for everything. God makes everything beautiful in its season, but unprofitable when taken out of time and place. There is a proper time and place for everything we do in our lives. I don't claim to be some spiritual giant but I do know God and I understand the concept of doing what I know is best for my family. Raising godly children is all about achieving the right balance between both their physical and their spiritual wellbeing.

A baby senses security. When you take special care to make sure your child is cared for properly, she will display a disposition that others will admire. It really is no mystery to the outcome of proper tender love and care. If she isn't fed and burped properly, changed when soiled, or held firmly and with confidence, she will whine and cry from discomfort.

I grew up in a family where we were given a plate of food prepared by the hands of a loving mother. Her expectation of me was that I eat what was placed before me. My mother knew the importance of a healthy, properly balanced meal. She didn't ask my opinion about what I thought was nutritious. When I became a mother, I also took great care to prepare those same types of meals for my children. This is so important to consider as mothers.

Unfortunately, the laziness and the fast-paced lifestyle of parents today is producing children who are unhealthy physically and emotionally. No wonder diabetes is at an epidemic proportion in our society. Before we can give our children a balanced life, we must also get our priorities in order about what is really important in our own lives.

Parents must make an honest assessment of what is truly important. Hopefully God and the welfare of your family are at the top of the list and take precedence over your careers and other interests.

Create a godly atmosphere in the home by keeping confusion or instabilities from your children. Providing security for your children allows them the freedom to focus on childish things, not problems that should be handled by the adults. Always be consistent in your love and respect for God before them. Never be hypocritical with your children, it causes them to adopt an unfavorable view of God.

I think that extracurricular activities and the demands on our children should be balanced so that your family life gives glory to God and is best suited for the whole family. Even when I worked a full time job, I remember eating together as a family every day of the week. We would discuss the day's events with our children. It gave my husband and me the opportunity to observe and talk to our children.

Providing structure is so vital to raising godly children. Statistics show that children who are actively involved in family activities are less likely to fall victim to deviant behavior. School and sports are important, but it is the parent's job to make sure that your children's lives are balanced and that they get the proper rest. Parents should realize that activities during the school week should be minimized and bedtime curfews should be enforced to make sure that your children get the required amount of sleep.

I thank God that we raised our children without the babysitting tool of the TV set. While TV can be a good form of entertainment, it isn't an alternative to effective parenting. I realized when my children were young, that what I put in them is what they would eventually become. I chose to raise them in a godly fashion and I thank God that I ended up with godly children.

RAISING CHILDREN THROUGH GOD

BRO. MICHAEL MEDEARIS

My wife, Angela, and I had been married for about two years when my daughter Deanna was born. I was the typical proud father and I thanked God for such a wonderful blessing. I did not understand however, that any previous notions I had about what it meant to be a father needed to be thrown out the window. I did not really know how to be a Christian father to my daughter. God knew that I would need the spiritual counsel and help of my wife. I also had the support of my church, like-minded Christian parents, and a pastor and a first lady who are role models.

Our pastor, Salem Robinson, Jr., used solid biblical principals and his own life to exemplify a Christian father. My growth and understanding of my role as a Christian father did not come overnight. After many parenting missteps, I've learned that you cannot raise a godly child unless you are first totally committed to being a godly parent. It is often said that children do not come with an instruction manual. The truth is that most people already own at least one copy of the greatest book on raising children ever written: the Holy Bible. I've learned that you must first apply its wisdom and insight to your own life before trying to use it to help you raise your child.

Every child is unique, but my daughter was gifted by the world's standards. Deanna started reading at an early age and she was able to hold a conversation with most adults before she was four. She skipped three grades, completed high school at age 16, and received seven scholarships for college. My daughter matured intellectually and physically long before she grew up emotionally and spiritually. At this point, you're probably thinking that my wife and I must have done a pretty good job raising our daughter. The truth is, we were caught up, even as young Christian parents, in many worldly notions about how a child should be raised.

Fortunately, God intervened in all of our lives. My daughter was married at an early age and soon got pregnant. The marriage did not last and she became separated from her husband before her daughter, Anysa, was born. We now look back on this as a blessing, because Anysa helped to keep her mother grounded in reality. I realized that my daughter may have grown up in the church, but she did not become a Christian until after she became an adult.

Deanna has now become a beautiful Christian and a sensitive young woman. I've had a lot of pleasure (and pain) watching her struggle to find meaning and purpose in her life. She has become an interesting and complex young woman. She's come through a difficult divorce and is a single parent, but through it all, she has kept a positive attitude and tenacity for living. I enjoy the lively conversations we have when we take opposing sides of an issue. I believe one of the reasons we get along so well and also get on each other's nerves is because we are so much alike.

My granddaughter, Anysa, was born on her mother's birthday. I am convinced that this was an omen of something special. There was a feeling of hope renewed when my granddaughter was born. Being a grandfather gives me the opportunity to do and say all those things I wanted to do for my own daughter. I was very close to my own grandfather and I have the same relationship with my granddaughter.

Anysa is very much like her mother, Deanna, and her grandmother, Angela, so I'm surrounded by three strong, passionate, and expressive Christian women. I spoil them while being spoiled at the same time, and I love every minute of it.

We are blessed that our daughter has been doing well on her own. She has an incredible job, is purchasing her own home, and is a wonderful Christian mother and role model. Angela and I had planned to be empty nesters once our daughter was grown, but the Lord had something totally different in mind.

Recently, my wife and I became the fulltime parents to a teenager named Lorenzo. We were his Court Appointed Special Advocates (CASA). CASA is a wonderful organization that provides a means for volunteers to become mentors and advocates for extremely abused and neglected children. Lorenzo has been a ward of the state in various institutions for many years. He was placed in a group foster home for boys for the last four years. I am thankful to his foster dad, Richard Washington, for giving Lorenzo a home during that time. It was crucial that Lorenzo find good foster home placement, otherwise he would have to grow up in residential treatment center. Most people don't realize that children need more than just food and a roof over their heads. Although our government institutions and social service organizations try to do the best they can to meet the needs of these children, they cannot replace the need for every child to feel they are a part of a family that loves them.

Although I now run our multimedia company, I used to work with kids as a tutor and instructional specialist through Book Boosters, a non-profit educational program my wife and I started over 20 years ago. I also worked with children with mental and emotional issues in our local school district and held a position as a youth instructor at our local 4-H organization.

I never realized how much I missed working with children until Lorenzo came to live with us. He provides me with the opportunity to perfect my Christian parenting skills and to continue working with troubled children, a talent the Lord has blessed me with.

I have learned that the key to joy and peace in the home comes when you are able to focus your time, energy, and effort on someone other than yourself. Though it may seem paradoxical, you must love yourself first before you can focus on others. I had to realize one day that being full of myself and doing what I wanted was not my purpose of my life. I thank God daily for the opportunity to be a Christian father, and for all the blessings and the love He has given me from my family.

GROWING UP AS A PREACHER'S KID

BRO. TIMOTHY ROBINSON

I'm a "PK," a preacher's kid. Many people think that preachers' kids are the bad kids. They are riotous, disobedient, and very disrespectful. This mindset doesn't apply to my little brother and me. I remember my dad sitting us down at an early age and telling us about the stereotypes surrounding preachers' kids and then informing us that was not going to be the case in this family. My parents love us dearly and have a love and fear for God that makes them want to please Him. It also helped them instill Christian character, respect, and that same love and fear for God in us that they have. We didn't learn our Christian values though physical or emotional abuse—it came from our parents' example.

My parents lived clean Christian lives before us. That helped lay a strong Christian foundation in our lives and once we got older, we didn't stray away from it.

I saw my dad get up every day and go to work and then come home and take care of our home. He is not a lazy man. I saw him love my mom with a gentle, unconditional, unwavering love that made me want to love my wife the same way. He is a real Christian man.

I saw my mom go to work and come home every day and have a balanced meal on the table for us to eat together as a family that evening. She is a virtuous woman. I saw her love and truly support my dad. Watching their example made me want a wife of my own that would love me the same way. I saw my parents live for Jesus without shame. They live an unspotted life outside the home and behind closed doors. I remember my dad always saying that we don't have any skeletons in our closets here. It's that unwavering Christian life that was lived before me every day that has made me the Christian man, father, and husband that I am today.

LIFE AS A YOUNG MOTHER

SIS. NEDIA ROBINSON

When I was asked to write about raising godly children I was very excited and couldn't wait to put my thoughts in black and white. However, as I began to contemplate what I would write, I became nervous at the idea and began to consider my qualifications on such a topic. My husband and I are the parents of a six year-old boy (with another baby on the way) whom we love dearly. Between the two of us, our actual "hands-on" parenting experience spans nearly seven years. Surely, I thought, there are others that could offer more years of enriching knowledge and experience!

As I sat and reflected on this topic, it occurred to me once again that when it comes to issues of living a Christian life, a major cornerstone of Christianity is pure and true faith. The scripture says that without faith it is impossible to please God. Therefore, as I travel on this journey of faith and motherhood, my ambition is to be a mother that is pleasing to my eternal Father.

I strive to show my child the ways of Jesus. My comfort comes in having the faith to believe that my Savior will provide me with the ability to be the parent my child needs. As a Christian mother, I find comfort in knowing that God has all things under control, even when I feel out of control.

My prayer as a mother is to prepare my son to critically think about his choices and to help him to make wise and godly decisions. I know he will eventually pave his own way, but as long as he's young enough for me to leave a lasting impression, I pray for the wisdom to guide and to direct him. I often talk with him about a variety of issues that he can relate to, as well as take these opportunities to teach him little lessons that I pray can help him make big decisions.

I try to reiterate the idea that just because the majority says something is right does not mean that it is right. I know as he gets older, he'll be confronted with peer pressure. But if he has a solid foundation about what is right and wrong in the sight of God, he'll be armed with the knowledge he needs. My hope is that he'll hesitate long enough to think about his actions and make a wise decision.

As my father-in-law (and my pastor) often says, life is about choices, and you have to live with the consequence of your decisions, whether it's good or bad. A scripture that comes to mind is Proverbs 31: 1–9, where King Lemuel speaks of the wisdom taught to him by his mother. She enlightened him on the actions that are not befitting to someone in his position. I find that these scriptures also apply to instructing our children today because we are heirs of our Father, the King, so our actions are to be honorable and upright. I love the way this mother explains to her son to stay away from "strong drink," in other words keep a sober mind, and don't allow your judgments to be diluted or disabled. This mother advised her son to be a man of integrity and honor at all times. She instructs him to judge righteously and defend the poor. These are all attributes that are of our Savior, Jesus Christ, and we are to be like him.

I remember listening to a scripture passage during a Sunday sermon from 2 Kings 4: 19–37 about a mother whose son had fallen ill and she had laid him in her lap until noon when he died in her arms. I will never forget this mother's unyielding and uncompromising struggle to find Elisha, the man of God, whom she knew could come and heal her dead child. Her husband questioned her request to seek Elisha so late in the day, but she continued on her quest. She ordered her servant to saddle the donkey and not to stop unless she directed him to.

When Elisha's servant approached to find out if everything was alright, she said that all was well and they kept riding. Her intentions were to find the man of God, whom she knew was anointed with the spirit of the Lord, so that he could come and heal her child. The scripture is beautiful because it shows the perseverance, love, and unyielding hope this mother had for her child and because of this faith, her child lived!

I truly admire the mother's strong and fervent faith! Her faith reflects that the godly child starts with a godly parent. How can we help our children if we have not been helped ourselves? How are we to teach our children about faith if we do not demonstrate it first? How is a child to truly learn without first being shown by their parents?

A Christian mother's love extends further than she ever thought possible. When others give up hope and their faith in God, the Christian mother clings to it with all her might. What others despise, the Christian mother will love and cherish. What a gift God gives to a Christian mother!

I still have a huge task ahead of me. But through prayer and faith in action, I know my God will be there guiding me and providing the light that I need and that He so lovingly and mercifully provides. I will forever be grateful for the opportunity that I've been given as a Christian mother. It is not only a blessing, but it is my duty to instruct my children in the ways of God, no matter how unpopular, outdated, or challenging it may be. It is what is expected and with His guidance it can be done!

It's amazing what motherhood has done for me. I feel so very blessed to be a Christian wife and mother. I pray for the wisdom that I need to help sustain my husband and family for years and years to come.

THE MAKING OF A MOTHER

SIS. DYNISHA COLE

I was born in Vicksburg, Mississippi. My mother and father divorced when I was about three years old. My mother worked a full time job, leaving my sister and I home most evenings after school and during the summers. She would ask the adult neighbors to watch our house and check on us. In spite of the hours she worked, she managed to attend most of my school events and stressed the importance of academic achievement.

Although I have some pleasant memories, most of my childhood was crowded with the pain of physical and emotional abuse, my parent's substance abuse, and their unresolved anger towards each other. I had my own secret battles with perversion and early childhood sex, lying, and eating disorders. I also felt pressured because of my family's high expectations of academic achievement.

From elementary through high school, I had several different intimate relationships. I did not attend church willingly. Upon graduating from high school, I attended college, pursuing a degree in biology. At the end of my first semester of college, I got pregnant and had an abortion. This was one of the most devastating events in my life. After that, I became entrenched in drinking, sex, and skipping class.

In 1998, I met the man who is now my husband, Mario Cole. Before we got married, I gave birth to our first son Jordan. Upon graduating, Mario accepted a job and moved to Arizona. Jordan and I stayed behind so that I could complete college. Raising Jordan alone and taking a full schedule of courses was quite difficult. I had to put Jordan in daycare and wasn't able to spend much time with him. Sometimes, I would take him to class with me just so that we could spend time together.

In 2001, Mario and I got married. Once I completed all of my courses except one, Jordan and I moved to Arizona with Mario. Because neither one of us were Christians at that time, the tensions grew between Mario and I, and we became detached. After Mario lost his job, we had to move into an income-based apartment. Soon after this, we had our second son, Marcus.

Exhausted and out of ideas, we decided to move from Arizona to Texas where my childhood friend resided. We stayed with her and her husband for about six months and slept on their floor while we were waiting for our new house to be built. It was during this period of time that I slowly fell into depression. Things did not get better between Mario and me. For the most part, we spent most of our days in arguments in the presence of the children.

Finally the house was complete. I worked a fulltime job during the day and a part-time job on the weekend. This did not give me a lot of time to spend with the kids. Mario began working at night while the children stayed home with him during the day. We were too busy working to be good parents to our children. In spite of all of these circumstances, I gave birth to our third son Joshua.

After being invited to church by a co-worker, I began attending Dunn's Memorial on a regular basis. In February 2005, I gave my life to Christ under the guidance of my spiritual father, Pastor Salem Robinson, Jr. He preached and set an excellent example of faith and obedience to the holiness of God through the gospel of Jesus Christ. Under this ministry, I began to understand the need for Christ in my life and the important role the Lord plays in having a functional family. In February 2006, my husband gave his life to Christ.

The women of the church demonstrated perfect godly character, and were excellent examples of holiness, humility, and service to God in Christ. First Lady Patricia Robinson shared her genuine commitment to righteousness as a godly mother and wife. Sister Angela Medearis' dedication and diligence in serving the Lord in her career, household, and church has had a great influence in my development. The sisterhood has had a great impact on my desire to improve as a mother. As a result of their examples, I'm learning that being a godly mother requires the power of God in Christ, sacrifice and commitment.

Now, when my husband and I correct or discipline our children, we've learned how to do it out of love, and not out of anger. All of the saints at Dunn's Memorial contributed considerably to my new life in Christ,

After recently being diagnosed with a hereditary disease, I face some of the toughest challenges in my faith. The continual encouragement of my pastor, my husband's dedication, my personal testimony, and the testimonies of the saints keep me going.

Since I've become a Christian mother, I try to take out time to look into my children's eyes and tell them that I love them. I remember the silent vow I made to God while they were in the womb, desiring to raise them before God. When I consider this vow, I often reevaluate my personal conviction in Jesus Christ, and see my need to grow closer to the Lord.

In order for me to be a true example of a Christian mother, I must rely on religion as a foundation. I face obstacles each day, from the time I wake up until I fall asleep at night. Satan uses all types of distractions to pull my attention away from valuable time that I could be spending spiritually and with the people that I love. I'm also motivated by the growth of my three sons and reflect on how I was raised as a child, and how I neglected my children while focusing on personal desires and other issues beyond my control.

Now, by the grace of God in Christ, I lean on Him to sustain me and protect my family in this uncertain world of sin. I realize that we can't succeed alone as parents and that we need God's Holy Spirit. His spirit helps us beyond our own abilities.

No matter what type of family a person is raised in or how many bad choices a parent makes in sin, in order to be successful, a parent needs a sure foundation in Christ.

A MOTHER'S HEART

SIS. DYNISHA COLE

FOR MY THREE SONS—JORDAN, MARCUS, AND JOSHUA

It's amazing how the hands of God work within a
    mother's heart!
He thumps the belly and pours the bones and names him
    from the start.
And when she walks, feeling the tiny feet within,
She knows that the pain of childbirth will soon begin.

She thanks the Lord for His blessings upon the sight
    of her beautiful son.
And stares in amazement at how his mouth, nose and eyes
Are as perfectly placed as the moon, sun and skies.
Oh how the hands of God work within a mother's heart!

Each day, she sets a Christian example and tells her sons
    about God's truth,
And shares with them about the sinful person that she was
    in her youth.
She tells them about the years that she lived in torment and in sin,
And how no one but God and Christ knew her heart and all
    the pain she held within.
It's amazing how the hands of God work within a mother's heart!

Each night, as the children sleep, the mother stops to reflect
About the woman she was before the word of God
Taught her about love, praise and respect.
It's amazing how the hands of God work within a mother's heart!

And when her sons are all grown men, and she is taking
    her last breath,
The godly truth she has instilled in them will not be erased
    by death.
She's raised three warriors for the Lord, now it's time for
    her soul to depart.
It's amazing how the hands of God work within a mother's heart!

Chapter Ten: Faith in Financial Freedom
ANGELA'S TESTIMONY

ost of our friends are entering retirement, but the Lord had a different plan for my husband, Michael, and me. We opened a new multimedia production company, (television, radio, film, animation, and publishing) and rapidly went broke. When we entered into this new venture, we didn't consider that God's plans and our plans might be in conflict. Every time we tried to direct the business the way we thought it should go, we hit a roadblock. Nothing seemed to be going right. Finally, our financial officer told us we needed to close the office, lay off our small staff, sell our office furniture and equipment, and declare bankruptcy! We didn't take his advice, but we did stop to evaluate why everything was going wrong.

Somehow, we'd deluded ourselves into thinking that it was all about us, and what we wanted to do. We'd forgotten how Christ had blessed us, and that we should serve Him and not ourselves. We soon realized that being successful in other aspects of our career had slowly blinded us to the will of God for our lives, and put our new company in jeopardy. We had fallen into a self-directed pattern that wasn't empowered by God. The more money we made, the less we prayed for guidance. The more successful we became, the more things we bought as evidence that the Lord was "blessing" us. The more we embraced the concepts of worldly success, the farther away we were drifting from what God calls successful. A success in the sight of God is a person who uses their talents to glorify Him in every aspect of their lives.

After our financial "wake-up" call, we underwent a spiritual overhaul. We turned our business over to the Lord, and rededicated our commitment to our faith. We've had many, many days when we didn't know how we were going to pay this or do that, but thank the Lord for the new-found faith we've developed! It has given us comfort knowing that in the darkest times, He will be our light.

Through it all, we've learned how the Lord can bring you through anything, if you truly lean and depend on Him. We've grown closer together as a couple, we've become more disciplined in every aspect of our spiritual, personal, and professional lives, and, most importantly, we've learned how to really pray.

Now, I've learned how to jump into the unknown by faith. I don't look down to see where I'm going to land when I take that daily leap. I've learned to look up to see how far I'm going to rise, because I know that the Lord isn't going to let me fall.

By faith, our business is blessed and directed by the will and the word of God. We have a financial freedom beyond what we ever possessed when we were successful by the world's standards. By faith, we've been able to use our business to create television and radio programs, and yes, even this book, so that we can glorify God and spread the gospel of Christ in a way that we never even dreamed of a few short years ago.

By faith, we've learned that God can multiply pennies, move strangers to help you, open doors that are cemented shut, close doors that don't need to be open, and fill you with the joy of knowing that He is in control and that you don't have to worry about anything as long as you remain steadfast.

By faith, we've learned that God's measure of success is done with a spiritual ruler not by the lines on a balance sheet or the amount in a bank account.

By faith, we've learned that God can turn a husband into a chief financial officer, a wife into an executive producer, a daughter into an editor, a grandchild into an animator, and a son into a source of inspiration. He can provide employees with the perfect skills at just the right time, do the absolute impossible with equipment that is outdated, and pull together a project that is glorious for all to behold.

By faith, we are able to live a wonderful life and help others to achieve the same spiritual blessings that we've obtained because we've learned to "jump." By faith, we've obtained financial freedom through our obedience to the word of God.

I know that the Lord will give us everything we need to continue to do the production work that we've come to love. I can't even express how excited I am about our future! Our lives, our marriage, our family, our financial situation, and our business is better than it ever was when were self-directed, self-absorbed, and blind to the will of God, and it has all been done by faith.

COMMENTS BY PASTOR SALEM ROBINSON, JR.

The key to financial freedom is having a heart that does the perfect will and the work of God. Keep in mind that God judges the intents and desires of our hearts. God weighs our motives more than our actions. If God did bless you with much, how much of a blessing would you honestly be to others? If you can answer that question truthfully, you may be on your way to financial freedom. Becoming financially free goes beyond just the elimination of debt but focuses more on living a life that's pleasing to God. It is about presenting your body a living sacrifice, holy and acceptable before God which is no more than what a Christian should be doing. Again, financial freedom is so much more than just money management and wealth building.

I know you're sick and tired of being sick and tired; but what you really mean is that you're tired of being broke. It seems every month you have the same worries and fears; too much debt, no real savings, and absolutely no budget or control over your life. Are you finally through telling yourself that this is normal, and that you're not the only one living like this? Do you really think that God wants His people to live this defeated life? Do you really want to know how to get out of this mess?

> But put ye on the Lord Jesus Christ, and make not provision for the flesh, to fulfill the lusts thereof. *Rom. 13:14*

Stop looking at a get-rich-quick scheme or planning to marry your way into riches!

> But they that will be rich fall into temptation and a snare, and into many foolish and hurtful lusts, which drown men in destruction and perdition. *1 Tim. 6:9*

A CHRISTIAN MARRIAGE AND MONEY

Did you know that it is important for Christians to save money? Did you know that a little change can add up to dollars? Would you believe that making changes in your money matters really matters? Did you know that your attitudes toward money are usually formed in childhood and have a direct impact on nearly every aspect of your life?

In a divorce-happy age, many surveys conclude financial issues are one of the leading causes of marital breakups. Are you really fighting about money? Deep problems like mistrust or resentment toward your spouse can surface through conflicts about money.

For example, some couples constantly fight over the amount of money the spouse has to pay to his ex-wife and kids for child support. The real truth is that the new spouse is angry that her husband isn't paying as much attention to the children from their union. On the surface, it looked like a money issue, but the underlying the problem was a much deeper one. Remember, it's not what the conflict is about that causes a breakup. It's how the conflict is handled.

WHAT IT MEANS TO BE FINANCIALLY FREE

Desiring the excessiveness of riches has more to do with selfish pride and the profitableness of acquired wealth than spiritual well-being. The lottery is not your ticket to riches if your final destination is heaven. Having the discipline and making the right choices to acquire wealth requires divine intervention. Keep in mind that you are the problem, not your money, and just getting more of it is not the solution.

While there are lots of financial experts and money geniuses out there, I'm not one of them. I've found that in order to experience financial freedom, you must start with simple faith and obedience to God's word. He will direct your path from there. If you are willing to make the sacrifices now that most people aren't willing to make, you are on your way to financial freedom.

The first step is to realize that you need to change your ways and then identify the obstacles that are in your way. Your untouchables or sacred cows that are draining you of every cent you earn but have a stronghold on your heart must be offered up for sacrifice.

> Thus saith the Lord of hosts; Consider your ways. *Hag. 1:7*

Again, the prophet Haggai is right on the money, pun intended! Now that we've said the obvious, let me tell you the key to financial freedom.

> Ye ask, and receive not, because ye ask amiss, that ye may consume it upon your lusts. *James 4:3*

Did you know that there are some people that cannot handle more than their daily bread because their hearts are not mature enough to receive it?

> Remove far from me vanity and lies: give me neither poverty nor riches; feed me with food convenient for me: Lest I be full, and deny thee, and say, Who is the Lord? or lest I be poor, and steal, and take the name of my God in vain. *Prov. 30:8–9*

> Owe no man any thing, but to love one another: for he that loveth another hath fulfilled the law. *Rom. 13:8*

This is how I got on the path to financial freedom as a young babe in Christ, even though I didn't really know it at the time. When I first made a profession of faith, I had just started a new job and a new marriage and needless to say, we struggled financially. Five years after accepting Jesus Christ, I was called to the ministry. I had a zeal to want to save the world!

On an evangelical outing in east Texas, I was given the opportunity to preach at a church, even though I had shown up at the services unannounced. I was filled with the love of God and a real care for the human soul, and the Lord spoke through me that day.

Afterwards, the pastor of the church stopped to talk with me. He was obviously impressed with my boldness and sincerity and maybe even filled with a little nostalgia. He shared something with me something that changed my life.

He said that he wished that he could speak that openly again about the word of God, but if he tried to preach that way now, he would lose favor with his congregation and most of all possibly lose his pension. He said that at his age, that was too great of a price to pay!

When I returned home I secluded myself in prayer and talked to the Lord. I remember asking the Lord to not let me end up like that minister. I told Him that I wanted to be financially independent in order to preach the purity of His Word without being held hostage financially by a congregation. I asked Him to help me to never allow money to be an issue in my ministry for Him.

I'm not sure exactly how long it took, but the Lord answered me in a very peculiar way. I was outside in the yard one evening and the Lord spoke to me and said, "I am going to make provision for you, trust in me."

I immediately dropped what I was doing ran into the house and shared with my wife what God had said to me. We both glorified God on His promise. My wife and I have lived to see God's words come to fruition in our lives. Whenever I'm reminded of God's deliverance, and believe me, financial freedom is deliverance, I feel so indebted to God.

Financial freedom is about having the courage to make sound decisions and the right choices. Always keep in mind that God empowers His will and His plans.

When we purchased our new home, I started out using my income alone to qualify and to budget from. I've lived my life by this rule of thumb. I found myself purchasing vehicles that we could afford rather than those that appealed to our selfish pride. When we opened our home to people less fortunate we made all of our resources available and God gave an increase to our substance.

When I seriously started planning for the future, I chose careers that did not conflict with my duties to God or my family. I made God and the spiritual welfare of my family my top objective in life. Every way that I turned in life was with the intent to give glory to God, and He has prospered my life. Even things that I didn't ask of God, He gave it to me, because I am committed to the work of the ministry.

Becoming financially free is tied directly to your spiritual commitment—God is the one that gives the increase.

> And God said to Solomon, Because this was in thine heart, and thou hast not asked riches, wealth, or honour, nor the life of thine enemies, neither yet hast asked long life; but hast asked wisdom and knowledge for thyself, that thou mayest judge my people, over whom I have made thee king. *2 Chron. 1:11*

Although I can't claim Solomon's riches, I can stake claim to some of his wisdom. Unknowingly, I made a choice as a young man to serve God rather than to go after the riches of this life. He has given me everything I need and more than what I even hoped for.

If you really want to experience financial freedom and never want to have to worry about the present or the future again, surrender your complete will to God and prepare yourself for a life of praise and thanksgiving.

DEBT-RELIEF FOR CHRISTIANS

- Develop a debt–free mind set. This comes down to will and determination. You must be fully committed in becoming debt free because it is the right thing before God.

- Establish a spending plan. This is essentially sitting down and developing a basic budget for the things you really need. Although the interest rates might be different, there is a psychological motivation to paying off small debts first and eliminating one debt after another.

- Consider earning additional income. The only caution here is to ensure that this doesn't cause tension or neglect to the family, and hinder you from serving God.

- Consider a radical change in your lifestyle. Having a problem with debt is often because we try to have too high of a standard of living, it is not always because we don't make enough income.

Pastor Robinson's Sunday School Lesson

Financial freedom is connected to your spiritual freedom. It has been said that the test of a man's character is how he spends his time and money. Biblical truths can give you a peace of mind with your finances. Without financial freedom, it is close to impossible to have real spiritual freedom. What could the people of God do for the kingdom of God if they were debt free?

We must not let money become overly important to us. Indeed, one of the first statements in Proverbs shows us we should honor God, who owns everything.

Prov. 3:9–10

9 Honour the Lord with thy substance, and with the first fruits of all thine increase:

10 So shall thy barns be filled with plenty, and thy presses shall burst out with new wine.

It is essential that we return a portion of what we receive to God. Also, how we go about earning our money is more important than how much we earn. Earn it in such a way that you can sleep at night (this should condemn all you lottery playing Christians!). God tells us, "The blessing of the Lord, it maketh rich, and he addeth no sorrow with it." (Prov. 10:22) We should earn our living honestly and not lie, cheat, or climb over the backs of others to make money.

Rom. 13:8

8 Owe no man any thing, but to love one another: for he that loveth another hath fulfilled the law.

This debt resolution applies carnally as well as spiritually.

Matt. 6:19–24

19 Lay not up for yourselves treasures upon earth, where moth and rust doth corrupt, and where thieves break through and steal:

20 But lay up for yourselves treasures in heaven, where neither moth nor rust doth corrupt, and where thieves do not break through nor steal:

21 For where your treasure is, there will your heart be also.

22 The light of the body is the eye: if therefore thine eye be single, thy whole body shall be full of light.

23 But if thine eye be evil, thy whole body shall be full of darkness. If therefore the light that is in thee be darkness, how great is that darkness!

24 No man can serve two masters: for either he will hate the one, and love the other; or else he will hold to the one, and despise the other. Ye cannot serve God and mammon.

Luke 16:10–12

10 He that is faithful in that which is least is faithful also in much: and he that is unjust in the least is unjust also in much.

11 If therefore ye have not been faithful in the unrighteous mammon, who will commit to your trust the true riches?

12 And if ye have not been faithful in that which is another man's, who shall give you that which is your own?

1 Tim. 6:17–19

17 Charge them that are rich in this world, that they be not highminded, nor trust in uncertain riches, but in the living God, who giveth us richly all things to enjoy;

18 That they do good, that they be rich in good works, ready to distribute, willing to communicate;

19 Laying up in store for themselves a good foundation against the time to come, that they may lay hold on eternal life.

Phil. 4:10–13

10 But I rejoiced in the Lord greatly, that now at the last your care of me hath flourished again; wherein ye were also careful, but ye lacked opportunity.

11 Not that I speak in respect of want: for I have learned, in whatsoever state I am, therewith to be content.

12 I know both how to be abased, and I know how to abound: every where and in all things I am instructed both to be full and to be hungry, both to abound and to suffer need.

13 I can do all things through Christ which strengtheneth me.

Acts 20:35

35 I have shewed you all things, how that so labouring ye ought to support the weak, and to remember the words of the Lord Jesus, how he said, It is more blessed to give than to receive.

The key to financial contentment and happiness is to share our blessings. Some of the most miserable people are those who cling to every last penny they have, fearful that someone else may get some of it. Some give freely, yet grow all the richer; others withhold what is due, and only suffer want. Do you give sacrificially to the Lord, or do you measure a small portion of your abundance as your offering? These saints stretched to the limit of what they could give:

2 Cor. 8:1–4

1 Moreover, brethren, we do you to wit of the grace of God bestowed on the churches of Macedonia;

2 How that in a great trial of affliction the abundance of their joy and their deep poverty abounded unto the riches of their liberality.

3 For to their power, I bear record, yea, and beyond their power they were willing of themselves;

4 Praying us with much intreaty that we would receive the gift, and take upon us the fellowship of the ministering to the saints.

Proverbs 27:20 reminds us that it's important to control our wants: "Hell and destruction are never full; so the eyes of man are never satisfied." Human nature is to always desire something. Once one want is fulfilled, our eyes will turn to something else. Have you ever heard this saying: "Some people spend money they don't have to buy things they don't need to impress people they don't like." Don't let material pursuits cause you to live a life of deceit and pretense. Lasting security is found not in a big bank account, but in building strength of character and a good reputation. No lasting security is to be found in wealth.

Prov. 11:28
28 He who trusts in his riches will fall, but the righteous will flourish.

So many unforeseen events can wipe out material wealth overnight—an accident or natural disaster, a stock market crash, an extended illness, or even a criminal act. The only lasting security is a righteous relationship with our Maker.

Prov. 11:4
4 Riches do not profit in the day of wrath, but righteousness delivers from death.

Becoming Financially Free

Sis. Ruby Nunn

Living for Christ in a Bible-believing and Bible-teaching church has made my life as a single Christian woman one of ease and true holy substance. "For my yoke is easy, and my burden is light," (Matt. 11:30). I have totally surrendered my life to Jesus Christ, my Lord and my Savior. Jesus has kept me in the hour of temptation. I am grateful for how the Lord takes care of me and shows me how much I am loved by God the Father and His Blessed Son, Jesus Christ. Therefore, my love for Christ has grown, and with this renewed love for my Lord and Savior my obedience to the word of God has been consistent and fervent.

In the beginning of 2006, I asked my pastor to pray with me. After almost 30 years in the school system, I desired to retire from teaching elementary school. I did not have nearly the money saved needed for retirement. I had lost the luster and the enjoyment for the job and was tired of the long commute. Teaching was no longer fun for me. My physical health was also being challenged. Going to work each day became harder and harder. I knew it was time for me to retire.

So how would I accomplish this, especially after just purchasing a new home only four years ago? I knew I needed to be free of all debts except for my mortgage. I paid off all my outstanding debts including my credit cards. I had lowered my credit limit so that I could pay off any balances without a carry over from month to month. I made a change in my life style. I kept my older model car when I paid it off, instead of getting a new one. I cut back on shopping or buying new clothes and for that matter, buying anything new. I was content with my manner of life.

It was amazing how God blessed me. I received a letter from the school district's retirement system office. A law had been passed allowing anyone who worked as a certified teaching assistant an entitlement to back pay and an additional year of teaching experience if it was done for two or more years. That same year I received additional monies from an injury that I sustained while on the job. I used that money to buy back the year I worked as a substitute and the years I worked for the state. This helped to increase my retirement allocation.

I knew from all this help that I had been given that the Lord had answered my prayer. I went forward with my retirement plans. Now, I know I need to be even more diligent in my giving to the Lord. So before I pay my bills I first set aside my offering to the Lord.

I also give to others. It makes me feel good that I'm able to share with others the blessings that God has given to me. My pastor calls this investing in the glory of God. He also says that the economics of investing in God's purpose pay great dividends.

I have been retired since May 31, 2006 and I love it. With the help of the Lord, I'm working on a plan to pay off my home mortgage. I have not made any other loans since 2002. I am truly counting down to financial freedom!

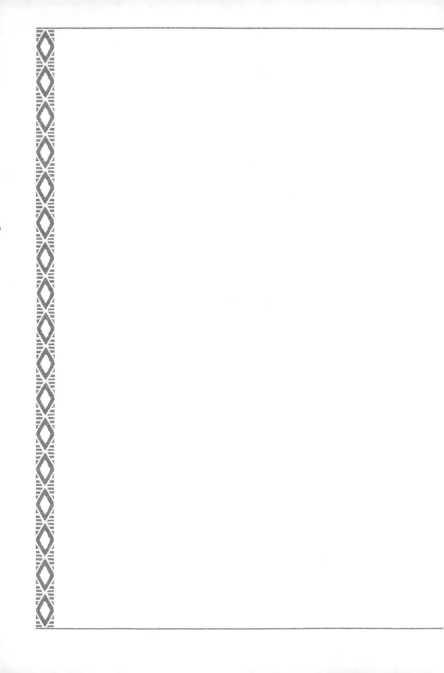

Epilogue
ANGELA SHELF MEDEARIS

THE FINAL INGREDIENTS

When I first started writing *Ten Ingredients for a Joyous Life and a Peaceful Home*, my goal was to create a book that would be a spiritual memoir about my life as a Christian. For more than a year, I've been able to meditate on the transformational power of Christianity and how it has shaped every aspect of my career as a writer, production company owner, and the host of "The Kitchen Diva!" television show. I've enjoyed the rare opportunity I've had to reflect on all the miraculous things that have happened to me since I accepted Jesus Christ on January 12, 1975.

There's no way I could write such a personal book without sharing some of the biblical concepts and Sunday School lessons that have been lived, preached, and taught by Pastor Salem Robinson, Jr. Pastor Robinson's spiritual leadership has spurred me to re-evaluate and strengthen my relationship with Jesus Christ, my husband, my family, and my friends. It was enlightening to review Pastor Robinson's Sunday School lessons and some of my favorite passages from the Bible from the perspective of an experienced Christian.

One of my favorite aspects of writing this book was discussing the ten ingredients of Christianity with my husband Michael, my daughter Deanna, and with Pastor and First Lady Robinson. Hearing their views about God's love, serving the Lord, forgiveness, friendship, overcoming fear, receiving healing, single Christian relationships, marital harmony, raising godly children, and becoming financially free was inspiring.

I thank the Lord for the opportunity to share the moving testimonies and the poetic talents of my Brothers and Sisters in Christ at Dunn's Memorial. Each testimony and poem has a special meaning because it has shown me that the Lord can give you the power to triumph over any situation and obstacle in your path.

I encourage you to take some time to quietly reflect upon the biblical concepts and lessons, and the words of wisdom contained in this book and apply them to your own life. I've learned from writing this book that it's a good thing to take an honest evaluation of your spiritual life, your words, and your deeds each day. Writing this memoir has strengthened my faith and re-doubled my determination to walk worthy of the blessing of salvation.

My prayer is that the contents of this book have inspired you, encouraged you to re-evaluate your relationship with Jesus Christ, and given you the boldness to share your testimony with others. May you also receive the strength that you need to carry you through life's daily challenges. I hope this book will also provide you with some spiritual "fuel" for your Christian journey and the tools you need to live a life filled with joy and peace.